Indispensable Companions:

Jesuit Brothers of the South
From Colonial Times to the Present

Jerome H. Neyrey, SJ

Indispensable Companions:

Jesuit Brothers of the South
From Colonial Times to the Present

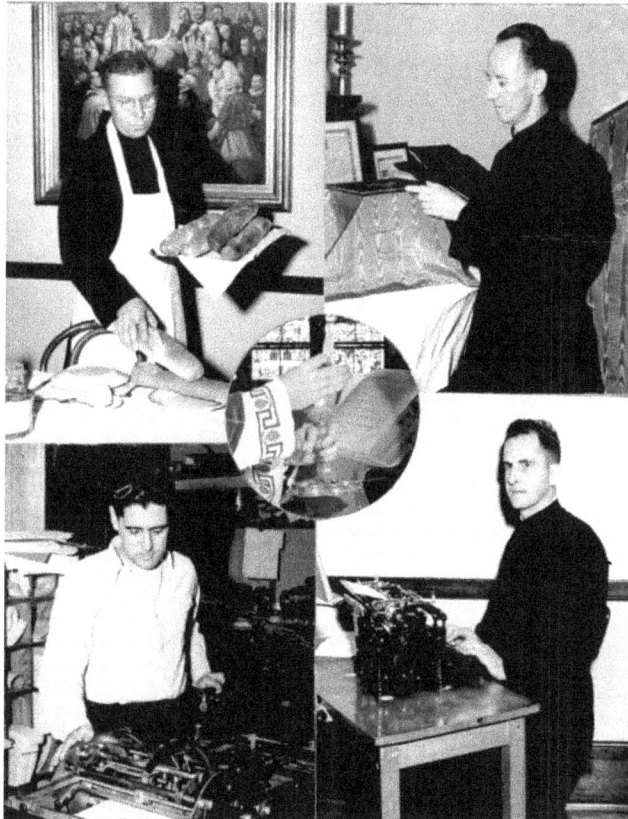

Jerome H. Neyrey, SJ

St. Alphonsus Rodriguez, SJ

HONOUR is flashed off exploit, so we say;
And those strokes once that gashed flesh or galled shield
Should tongue that time now, trumpet now that field,
And, on the fighter, forge his glorious day.
On Christ they do and on the martyr may;
But be the war within, the brand we wield
Unseen, the heroic breast not outward-steeled,
Earth hears no hurtle then from fiercest fray.

Yet God (that hews mountain and continent,
Earth, all, out; who, with trickling increment,
Veins violets and tall trees makes more and more)
Could crowd career with conquest while there went
Those years and years by of world without event
That in Majorca Alfonso watched the door.

                                    - Gerard Manley Hopkins, SJ

St. Alphonsus Rodriguez speaking with St. Peter Claver

Stained glass from the Jesuit Community Chapel,
Jesuit High School, New Orleans

Acknowledgments:

John T. Landry
Executive Producer

Enzo's Publications
Photography, Layout & Production Manager

Archival Assitance:

Joan Gaulene
Archives of the Former New Orleans Province

Mary Struckle
Archives of the Former Missouri Province

Elizabeth Cook
Regis College Archives

Associate Editors:

Edward B. Arroyo, SJ
Keith Guidry
Francis W. Huete, SJ
Thomas J. Madden, SJ
Richard McGowan, SJ
Leo A. Nicoll, SJ

ISBN - 13:978-0692620281

November, 2017

"Create Space"   www.createspace.com

A Special Debt of Gratitude to These Who Provided Financial Assistance

Donald Bollinger
New Orleans, La

Richard C. Broussard
Lafayette, La

Dwayne David
Lafayette, La

William Keaty, DDS
Lafayette, La

Keith and Noel Landen
Franklin, La

John T. Landry
Abbeville, La

Bret Lofton
Lafayette, La

B.I. Moody III
Crowley, La

J. Jerome Smith. DDS
Lafayette, La

Richard E. Zuschlag
Lafayette, La

Table of Contents

Honor Roll

List of Jesuit Brothers acknowledged by the Church as Saints, Blesseds, Venerables, and Servants of God

(Joseph Tylenda, *Jesuit Saints and Martyrs*, 2nd ed., 1998 pp 463-472)

Ferdinand Álvares

Francis Álvares

Gaspar Álvares

Manuel Álvares

Francis Aranha

John Baptist Arconada

Ralph Ashley

Alphonsus de Baena

Ferdinand Bonacina

Mark Caldeira

James de Carvalho

Dominic Collins

Simon de Costa

John de La Lande

Ignatius Elduayen

Gregory Escribano

Ambrose Fernandes

Anthony Fernandes

Dominic Fernandes

Peter Fernandes

Joseph Mark Figueroa

Peter Fontoura

Dennis Fujishima

Francis Gárate

Peter Gelabert

René Goupil

Raymond Grimaltos

Haïdar Habeiche

Dominic Ibarlucea

Philip Iriondo

Lawrence Isla

Vincent Kaun

James Kisai

Leonard Kimura

Peter Kinsei

Paul Kinsuke

John Kisaku

Joseph Llatje

Habib Maksoud

Constantine March

John de Mayorga

James de Montalbán

Michael Nakashima

Peter Onizuka

Augustine Ota

Nicholas Owen

Francis Paulo

Bras Ribeiro

Alphonsus Rodríguez

Pascual Ruiz

Gaspar Sadamatsu

Vincent Sales

William Saultemouche

Joseph Sampol

Anthony Sanchiz

Joseph Tarrats

Michael Tozo

Amaro Vas

Simon Yempo

Elias Younès

John de Zafra

Stephen Zuraire

Brothers who were painters:

Jean Denis Attiret
Bernardo Bitti
Emmanuel Pereira
Daniel Seghers
Giuseppe Castiglione
Ignatius Sichelbart
Antonio Moscheni
Martin Coronas Pueyo

Brothers who were architects:

Luca Bienni
Pieter Huyssens
Jean du Blocq
Giovanni Baptista Primoli
Andrés Bianchi
Giuseppe Castiglione
Eulaio Morales
Theofile Roelandt
Polydor Verbrugge
Ignatius Scoles

Brothers who were both Painters and Architects

Andreas Pozzo (1642 – 1709)

Jesuit Brother Artists of the South

Architects:

Cornelius Otten
(St. Charles Borromeo in Grand Coteau, La;
St. Joseph in Macon, Ga;
Sacred Heart in Tampa, Fla)

Joseph Brinkhaus
(Belfry, St. Charles Borromeo)

Painter, ceramics:

Julien Rivet

Painting, sculpture:

Gebhardt Fröhlich

Crucifix
by
Brother Gebhard Fröhlich, SJ

Introduction

How to Think about the Jesuit Brother

To appreciate the vocation of the Jesuit Brothers in the South, we need to know their narrative from the time of the founding of the Society until now. We possess an un-published history of the Jesuits of the South by Michael Kenny, SJ (*Jesuits in Our Southland* 1566 – 1946), who tells much of this narrative story. Also important are the annual catalogues of the Lyons Province, the Independent New Orleans Mission, and finally the New Orleans Province, and especially the archives housed in the library of Loyola University in New Orleans, which provide year-by-year, place-by-place and job-by-job information about each Brother. From these catalogues, moreover, we learn the population of the New Orleans Jesuits year-by-year and the ratio of brothers to priests for nearly two centuries.

Jesuit priests are generally in public teaching classes, preaching and celebrating the sacraments. But in the past, people rarely saw Jesuit Brothers because priests and brothers had different tasks and assignments: priests were public figures and brothers ensured that the priestly ministry happened at home. Both are genuine Jesuits; both pronounce the same vows; both have the same spiritual life. Put simply, Brothers are Jesuits – complete in every way, except in governmental functions of the Order. The biographies in this volume represent all the Jesuit Brothers who labored in Louisiana, the rest of the South, Texas, New Mexico and Colorado. Often there is little documentation on individual Brothers, but we treasure their names, their places of origin, their grave sites and their service to the apostolate.

Brothers in the Early Society

Although St. Ignatius founded a "priestly order," it became immediately apparent that if the priests were to do their ministry outside of the house or church, "coadjutors" or assistants were needed to build and maintain these institutions, as well as to provide for the necessities of daily living. Thus a mere six years after the founding of the Society (1540), Ignatius petitioned for and received papal approval to include spiritual and temporal coadjutors as full-status members of the Order. Although the aim of all Jesuits is to "aid" or "help" souls, the term "coadjutor," which means "co-helper," was borrowed from Vatican parlance to identify Jesuits who helped, but either did not take solemn vows, namely, spiritual coadjutors or who labored for the support and maintenance of Jesuit houses, namely temporal coadjutors or Brothers. The difference between the two types of coadjutors was defined this way in the Constitutions: "It is more characteristic of the spiritual coadjutors to aid the Society by hearing confessions, giving exhortations, and teaching Christian doctrine. … It is more characteristic of the temporal coadjutors to exercise themselves in all the low and humble services which are enjoined on them" (114). These services are later enumerated in the same document: "Such are ordinarily, in large houses, the occupations of a cook, steward, buyer, doorkeeper, infirmarian, launderer, gardener, and alms-gatherer" (149). Thus from the beginning, Priests and Brothers were Jesuits first and foremost; their training and tasks, however, were different. One of the premier Jesuit historians, John W. O'Malley, SJ, profiles the Jesuit Brother in the time of the founding of the Society of Jesus:

> Class distinction was not altogether eliminated, even for actual members of the Society. The "temporal coadjutors" (or lay brothers) came from respectable and stable social origins – sons of artisans (40 percent), peasants who owned their own land (25 percent); or small merchants (12 percent). They came into the Society, therefore, either with some practical skill or with the intention of learning one. They for the most part functioned as cooks, tailors, gardeners, buyers, masons, carpenters, even architects, and in other ways helped in "temporalities," even most essential as communities grew larger. In the sixteenth century they contributed about 25 percent of the Society's total membership (John W. O'Malley, *The First Jesuits*, 60).

The Brothers who were drawn to Jesuit religious life would have been similar to Benedictine, Franciscan, and Dominican monks who farmed, cooked, wove cloth, etc. in their monasteries. This first generation of Brothers were artisans, workers in wood and iron, masons and carpenters, painters and architects and were capable in the essential tasks of building and maintaining an institution. Literacy rate at this time would have been low, but it is a safe assumption that many Brothers had basic or craft literacy. In the *Constitutions* of the Order, the following was stated: "Neither ought he (a Brother) to seek more learning than he had when he entered" (117.6); but later Jesuit General Congregations cancelled this. As the ministry of the Society of Jesus grew and expanded, the need for Brothers became acute. The larger the school, the more Brothers needed to run it.

Brothers in the South

Brothers belonged to the first team of Jesuits to labor in Louisiana. Alas, much of what we know of them is in "asides," as priestly ministry was the focus of the earliest records. But any mention is all the more important. The following paragraphs, all taken from Michael Kenny's *Jesuits in Our Southland,* are listed chronologically.

In Father deBeaubois' first band were Fathers Paul du Poisson, John Souel, and Brother Philip de Crucy. These he assigned to their various posts, and on May 28, 1727, all four pirogued up the river from New Orleans. It took thirty days to reach the first destined post … resting a few days at Natchez, they arrived at Yazoo June 23, and leaving Father Souel at his assigned mission there, they continued up the river to the Arkansas post. Parting with Father Dumas who went up to Illinois, Father Du Poisson, with Brother de Crucy, took up his station with the French garrison and the four Arkansas tribes.

This Brother has a name, Philip de Crucy, but what he did is left to our imagination. One can easily imagine Brother de Crucy, not only paddling the pirogue, but making a camp and cooking meals for his fellow travelers. Father Du Poisson insisted on a "church" in every village, which, of course, would have been left to Brother de Crucy to erect. Eventually this faithful Jesuit succumbed to toil and climate and died shortly after, in 1728.

In 1738, in a letter to Father General in Rome, Fr. Mathurin Le Petit, SJ remarked: "Here in New Orleans we count two priests, living with *two lay brothers*" (Kenny, 20). Neither brother is named. We wait for the next mention of a Jesuit brother in Louisiana until the Restoration of the Society of Jesus after 1814. Antoine Blanc, Bishop of New Orleans, persuaded Father General Roothaan in a face-to-face conference to send Jesuits to open a college in Louisiana. On Christmas Eve 1836, six fathers and two brothers sailed from Le Havre, reaching New Orleans February 22, 1837" (Kenny, 32). The brothers are nameless, but so are the priests.

The college they founded in Grand Coteau, La briefly became the charge of the Missouri Mission. When restored to the Southern Jesuits in 1844, the staff of Grand Coteau "included Fathers Sautois, Parret, d'Hoop, Parmando, Van Hulst, Mearns, and Treyens … and a considerable reinforcement of *very sociable lay brothers*" (Kenny, 41). Funny how Brothers tend to lose their names. On May 17, 1848 Father Schmidt and Brothers Clement Staub and Anthony Kramer arrived in New Orleans to labor at the new college being built. In 1849, "with the aid of Clement Staub and Ignatius Boemecke and other efficient lay brothers, Rev. Hippolyte Gache, first pastor and president, had the frame buildings for the new college ready for opening January 2, 1850."(Kenny, 53).

In the same year, Bishop Blanc put the church of St. Michael in Convent, La in the charge of Jesuits: he appointed Ladavière "permanent Pastor and Rector of St. Michael's at Convent … (including) two priests and *a lay brother* (unnamed)" (Kenny, 43).

The Jesuits sought to establish a school in Baton Rouge, La, which survived with difficulty. The Enemy of Enemies, yellow fever, decimated their numbers. "On October 7, 1853 *Brother Henry Visconti*, a qualified physician, who had spent twenty-seven of his sixty years in the Society, mostly as infirmarian, and had given his skilled services to the sick with great generosity, shared joyously in the same reward (yellow fever)" (Kenny, 54). *Brother Corné* was the trusty support of the Fathers in Baton Rouge and was himself a fruitful missionary by religious example and devoted service. He is catalogued variously as buyer, baker, farmer, builder, carpenter. But more descriptively *ad omnia*, which is translated as: "available for all assignments." Brother Philip Corné was called to his reward at Baton Rouge October 28, 1862 in the sixty-third year of his age and 45th of religious life. The catalogue of the New Orleans Mission of the Lyons province for 1869 lists thirty-five priests, a scholastic, and *thirty-three coadjutor brothers.*

In 1872 Father Joseph Heidencamp, Alexis de Stockalper, Aloysius Boeni, and Alexander Friend, and in 1873 Emmanuel de la Morinière, Alfred Blatter, Henry Rigues (a Confederate veteran) and *Brothers Steiner, Zuber and Amacker* were posted to Grand Coteau.

Pio Nono, an existing institution in Macon, Ga, was being transformed into a Jesuit Novitiate, named St. Stanislaus Koska. Father Butler took formal possession of it on March 7, 1887, and he brought *Brothers Andrew and Anthony Albert* to put house and place in order … living conditions seemed quite satisfactory to the fourteen Juniors from Florissant and the eighteen novices who followed the ensuing weeks. There were *twenty-two coadjutor novices*, of whom ten were brought from Spain by Father Tyrell (Kenny, 139).

In 1884, Father Butler finally acceded to the request of Bishop Aloysius Gallagher to operate a college in Galveston and its adjacent church.

> The new rector, John O'Connor, transformed the college's large hall into a serviceable chapel with the expert aid of *Brother Otten*. When the Jesuits took over the college, a large church was already planned by Nicholas J. Clayton. A devoté of medieval architecture, he chose French Romanesque. His ambitious designs made his work expensive, but this Father Butler could control. … The expense was also much reduced by the builder, *Brother Cornelius Otten, SJ*, an architect of like mind, who was also a master of every trade and craft.

Joseph Brinkhaus, chief coordinating head, with *de Volder, Garbely, Morge, and Soto*, began work on a second Jesuit church in New Orleans, the "Little Jesuits Church." It should be distinguished from the great Jesuit Church on Baronne Street. This new church was a genuine Louisiana product: the wood used came entirely from this state; the stained glass windows were locally produced. Jesuit Brothers did the hand-carving and carpentry work, using plans drawn by Nicholas Clayton of Galveston. Its size was 130' x 60'. On May 29, 1892, Holy Name was solemnly blessed and dedicated to the honor and glory of God.

In 1918 an impressive replacement for the initial wooden church occasioned the transferral of the old "Little Jesuits" building safely across the Mississippi to Westwego, a testimony to the quality of workmanship of the brothers who built it. Renamed Our Lady of Prompt Succor, it continued to host a parish congregation for decades. Brinkhaus entrusted to cabinet artists the task of serviceable and elegant work. Examples of this artistry remain in Loyola and in many sacristies and churches of the province (Kenny, 163).

Contagious Vocations: Boemecke – Hugh – Maring – Rittmeyer

A Clan of 15 Uncles, Brothers and Cousins

Ignatius, the eldest of many Boemeckes, was born on August 1, 1825. Plying his trade as carpenter, he traveled from Germany and arrived in Rome in 1847. Ignatius met Father General Roothaan, who showed such interest in this sterling Catholic Hanoverian that when Ignatius asked for admission into the Society, he was received on June 19, 1847. Father Roothaan promptly suggested that he join the band of Jesuits whom Father Curioz was assembling for the New Orleans Mission. And so he came to the American South. The remainder of his biography may be found in the chronology of Jesuit Brothers 1831-1888.

It is likely that Father Augustine Hugh caught the Boemecke Jesuit virus, for he entered the Order at the same time as the three Brothers Boemecke. Another member of the clan, Fr. Henry Maring, re-established the college in Grand Coteau, and then succeeded to the presidency of the college in New Orleans, where he was subsequently treasurer and consultor of the Mission till his death March 24, 1930, his sixty-eighth year of age and fiftieth year of Jesuit Life.

The Marings came from Witten on the Ruhr. Father Henry brought out of Witten two Maring nephews, who perpetuated worthily the family traditions, Father Karl at Loyola University and Marine Chaplain Joseph in the far Pacific. Their Rittmeyer cousins, Fr. George, a veteran professor of philosophy who died in 1924, and Brother Henry, his worthy brother in Religion as in blood, were natives of Nesselroeden. They number fifteen good Jesuits of three generations in every service of the province, all descendants of one loyal Catholic couple in the Protestant-encircled villages of Catholic Nesselroeden (Kenny, 158-59).

The Brothers, Year-by-Year and Place-by-Place

The catalogues of the Lyons province and especially the archives at Loyola University allow us to dig a bit deeper into the lives and works of the Brothers. We have chosen to report on Brothers at certain times and at specific institutions.

The catalogue for 1866 lists the following Brothers working at Spring Hill College, Mobile, Ala:

COADJUTORES (Latin word for "BROTHERS")

Adrianus Lagger, *Credent* (refectorian)
Aloisius Schmidt, *Infirm*   (infirmarian)
Andreas Boëmecke, *Janit, Sart, Cust. vest. NN*   (porter, tailor, keeper of the Jesuits' clothing)
Antonius Krammer, *Arment*   (in charge of the horses and mules)
Caesar Gentinetta, *Pist* (baker)
Clemens Staub, *Lamp* (lamplighter)
Franciscus Imfeld, *Hortul* (groundskeeper)
Franciscus Imsand, Stab   (in charge of the barn)
Joannes Mengus, *Villa* (in charge of villa)
Josephus Garbely, *Ad omnia* (available for any assignment)

Josephus Jensch, *Adj. Infirm* (assistant infirmarian)
Leo Sengghen, *Arment* (in charge of horses and mules)
Paulus Viboux, *Cust. vest. alumn* (keeper of the students' clothing)
Philippus Schmidt, *Empt* (buyer)
Stephanus Walter, *Ad omnia* (available for any assignment)\

PP. 11 — Schol. 3 — Coadj. 15

We begin with the bottom line of the above list: at this point, Spring Hill College housed more brothers than priests (15 vs 11). When we examine what these brothers did, it is clear that they provided the food and the serving of the food; moreover, they cared for the sick in the community and among the students as well; it may be that the brothers were in charge of food production, for two of them were in charge of the mules and horses, as well as the barn. They managed the buying of goods and supplies for the college. And two brothers were assigned *ad omnia*, that is, to whatever tasks needed to be done – jacks of all trades. In short, the college could not operate without the competent management of the Brothers.

Let us consider another catalogue of Brothers, this time those listed at St. Charles College, Grand Coteau, in 1876.

Andreas Albert, *Aedit., Ad omnia* (sacristan, available for any job)
Andreas Boëmecke, *Janit, Sart* (porter, tailor)
Antonius Kramer, *Arment* (manager of the storeroom of common items)
Franciscus Imfeld, *Credent* (refectorian)
Franciscus Imsand, *Adj. Coq* (assistant cook)
Joannes Mengus, *Hortul* (groundskeeper)
Joannes Samuel, *Fab, Ad omnia* (carpenter, available for any assignment)
Josephus Ducret, *Adj. proc* (assistant treasurer)
Josephus Garbely, *Arcul* (cabinetmaker)
Paulus Viboux, *Cust. vest, Soc. exeunt* (keeper of the Jesuits' clothing; companion
                              to those with ministry outside the college)
Philippus Schmidt, *Empt* (buyer)
Vincentius Blatter, *Coq* (cook)
Adrianus Lagger, *Stab* (in charge of the barn)

The domestic tasks were typically covered: tailor, cook, refectorian, treasurer, carpenter, keeper of the clothing, and buyer. But the farm aspect of the college, i.e., the growing of foods, husbandry of the college's animals, and all aspects of sowing and reaping, appear to have been in the charge of laymen from the area. This array of tasks performed and not performed at Grand Coteau is identical with the roster of tasks assigned to brothers at Spring Hill College.

It will surely be helpful to compare the roster of brothers who in 1877 were working at St. Charles College in Grand Coteau with those employed at Spring Hill College in Mobile.

St. Charles College 1877	Spring Hill College 1877
Antonius Müller, sacristan, porter, tailor	Adrianus Lagger, cook
Clemens Hagan, available for whatever is needed	Andreas Albert, available for whatever is needed
Cornelius Otten, cabinetmaker, available for domestic jobs	Andreas Boëmecke, porter, tailor, sacristan
Franciscus Zuber, infirmarian, baker	Clemens Hagan, asst. cook
Hermanus Hugh, apprentice cabinetmaker	Franciscus Imfeld, refectorian
Joannes King, clothing manager, buyer	Franciscus Xaverius Amacker, infirmarian
Joannes Steiner, cook, manager of room for personal items	Johannes Samuel, carpenter, manager of room for personal items
Josephus Brinkhaus, assistant cabinetmaker	Josephus Ducret, assistant treasurer
Josephus Strebel, keeper of the wine cellar	Josephus Garbely, in charge of mules and horses
Raymundus Alier, chief refectorian, keeper of wine cellar	Paulus Viboux, keeper of the community's clothing
Simeon Sauzeat, companion of Jesuits with ministry outside the college	Philippus Schmidt, library worker, companion of Jesuits with ministry outside the college
Vincentius Blatter, manager of the barn, available for local tasks	Clemens Staub, sacristan, cook, companion of Jesuits with ministry outside the college

Brother Lloyd Barry, SJ of the New Orleans Province wrote a brief description of the Brother vocation, "**What is a Brother,**" which captures its maturation long before the recent general congregations of the Order, which makes it all the more significant for the ways in which the Jesuit Brother would be described and valued. Because of the historical nature of Barry's remarks, we quote him in full:

Let me start by asking a question.

What is the Jesuit Brother? The Jesuit Brother is many things.

- He is the refrigeration mechanic and electrician at Jesuit High School in New Orleans.
- He is the treasurer at Jesuit High in Dallas.
- He is the man in charge of the boilers and parking lot at Jesuit High in Shreveport.
- Yes, he is also the man who teaches Art at Spring Hill College.

These are but a few of the things that the Jesuit Brother is … However before he is any one of these things he is a JESUIT in the full sense of the word. The Brother Engineer, the Brother Cook and the Brother Sacristan, SJ are as truly JESUITS as are the Father Pastor, the Father Confessor and the Father Instructor.

The Motivation that all Jesuits share is the same: For the Greater Glory of God and for the Salvation of Souls. They dedicate their lives to the service of Christ's church both at home and in the Foreign Missions.

So you see, the term JESUIT describes the Brothers as well as it does the Scholastics (that is, candidates for ordination), and Priests, whom you know so well.

Bearing in mind what I have already said, I believe we are now in a better position to answer the question: What is a Jesuit Brother?

The Jesuit "Brother" is a man – a Catholic – who has given himself, his talents, his work, and his prayers to the service of the Church by VOWING to observe the Evangelical Counsels: POVERTY, CHASTITY, and OBEDIENCE according to the Constitutions of the Society of Jesus.

Men who want to be Jesuit Brothers vary widely in AGE, INTERESTS, and EXPERIENCE. Some come right out of high school, business, college, while others come after a few or many years of work in the occupation of their choice. … But all who come are men who feel that God is calling them to His service as Jesuits and who have the Courage and Generosity to say YES.

One seemingly insignificant change was made in the province catalogue for 1970. Up to that time, when the members of a particular house were listed, first came the fathers, then separately the scholastics and finally the brothers. And in the summary index of Jesuits at the end of the catalogue, again the Jesuits were separated into priests, scholastics and brothers. But in 1970, all members of a given house began to be listed together, alphabetically; and in the summary index of the members of the whole province, the brothers are merged with the rest and listed, not by grade, but in a truly inclusive way, namely, alphabetically.

The Ministry of the Order Requires the Service of the Brothers

The work of the Jesuit Brothers is as varied as the temporal needs of the members of their religious community. Their service as cooks, bakers, buyers, and refectorian is invaluable in providing meals for the community. As tailors, cobblers, and superintendents of the community laundry, the Brothers contribute to the clothing of the members of the Order. As painters, carpenters, and plumbers they make the repairs and provide the accommodations necessary for a well-functioning community. Skilled Brother engineers, mechanics, and electricians manage the heating and refrigeration of Jesuit institutions. They tend to the upkeep of cars and trucks owned by the various communities.

Just how indispensable the Brothers are to the Order will become clearer if we examine their work under the aspect of money-saving. Suppose, for instance, that monthly checks had to be paid out to hired engineers and electricians. Suppose that each and every piece of plumbing, carpentry, painting, tailoring and cobbling meant a bill for payment from the community treasury … the paid services of a trained nurse replaced the gratis administrations of the Brother infirmarian in caring for the sick of the community. Finally, suppose the monthly payroll included wages for porter, a chauffeur, a sacristan, who performed the duties of a Brother porter, a Brother chauffeur, Brother Sacristan. In the light of finances the work of the Lay-Brother becomes a real necessity.

Then there is the element of religious influence which lifts the labors of the religious Brother over similar work performed by hired help. It is quite desirable that the religious community be a source of spiritual good in every possible way. This end is more efficaciously attained when the temporal affairs of the institution are in the hands of men consecrated to God. … The Brother truly shares the apostolate of the Jesuit priest. The letters which the Brother stenographer writes, the sewing, cobbling, plumbing, repair work, etc., of the Brothers – all contribute directly or indirectly to the salvation of souls. The spirit in which these multifarious works are performed sanctify the

Brother's own soul ("The Training of a Jesuit – The Jesuit Brother," pp. 3-5 in *The Southern Jesuit*, November 1935).

Vocation Poster Illustrating Typical Ministries of the Brothers

Jesuit Brothers at the 36th General Congregation

For the first time ever, Jesuit brothers have been chosen to be electors at a General Congregation. One of them, moreover, was the youngest elector at the Congregation. **James Edema**, 39-year-old counselor from Uganda, was elected by the Jesuit Conference of Africa. The Australian **Ian Cribb**, the oldest elector at the age of 66, was elected by the Conference of Asia Pacific. His theological specialy is spirituality The Jesuit Conference of Canada and the United States, for its part, chose Brother **Guy Consolmagno** who, at 64, is an astronomer with a Ph.D. in Planetary Science and is the current director of the Vatican Observatory. Brother Consolmagno, a well published author, is interested in the intellectual apostolate, especially the relationship between faith and science. The 54-year-old Brother **Stephen Power** from England was elected by the Conference of Europe. His ministry is the social apostolate, especially the Jesuit Refugee Service, and has worked in London, Sudan, and Kenya. The Jesuit Conference of Meridional Asia elected a 51-year-old educator from India, Brother **Thomas Vaz**, the Coordinator of the Education Sector of his home province, Mumbai. Brother **Eudson Ramos**, who at 42 years of age is the current socius for the provincial of Brazil, was elected by the Conference of Latin America. He has worked as an administrator and vocations promoter. Although brothers have participated in past General Congregations, this is the first time they did so as electors.

Prayer for Generosity

Teach me to be generous,
Teach me to serve you as you deserve,
To give and not to count the cost,
To fight and not to heed the wounds,
To labor and not to seek for rest,
To sacrifice with no prospect of reward
Save knowing that I have done your will.

The Colonial Period
[1700 – 1763]

With the founding of New Orleans, the first period of the history of the Jesuit Brothers in the South begins. But the Order had many enemies, among them the Capuchin Friars who staffed the cathedral and considered the arrival of the Jesuits as encroaching on their pastoral work, which was not the case, since all Jesuits in Louisiana in those days undertook missionary work with the native Indian tribes, not parochial expansion. Thus, there should not have been competition between the two religious orders. Eventually on February 10, 1726 a satisfactory agreement was reached between Bienville and Fr. Charlevois, SJ. The Brothers were not mentioned by name in this, but their presence and skills were essential to make the agreement work. According to the conditions of the agreement, the Jesuits must supply a minimum of 14 missionaries for all Louisiana (from Great Lakes to Gulf), to provide a chapel, presbytery at their own expense, and cede all lands on the west of the river. The sole purpose of the plantation which resulted was to support the missionaries who traveled to the various Indian tribes and dwelt among them.

Fr. Ignatius de Beaubois, SJ, returned to New Orleans with a royal approval; he brought with him six fathers and one brother. He was joined in August of 1727 by three Jesuits who had left France to conduct the Ursulines on their long voyage to Louisiana. de Beaubois immediately sent these three priests and the brother on their mission up the river to the native Indian tribes. All four have names, in particular Br. Philip de Crucy, SJ. We have no description of what labors a brother would do in this mission, but one may imagine that the brother provided shelter, hunted for food and cooked meals, and generally whatever needed to be done to support the mission.

Kenny (p. 14) describes the labors of Paul du Poissson, SJ; a considerate reader will know that such labors of a priest would be impossible without the assistance of a brother:

> "Traversing by pirogue and afoot the several leagues that separated the villages, he would settle down for some days in each, instructing children and adults, holding prayer meetings, caring for their wounds and diseases and other needs and rendering skillfully every possible physical and spiritual assistance."

A letter of 1738 from Mathurin Le Petit, SJ to Father General Retz writes, "Here in New Orleans we count two priests, living with *two lay brothers*."

Entrusting Myself to the Hands of Jesus

I've come to think that the only,
the supreme, prayer we can offer up
during these hours when the road
before us is shrouded in darkness,
is that of our Master on the cross:

Into your hands I commend my spirit.

To the hands that broke and gave life to the bread,
that blessed and caressed, that were pierced,
to the kindly and mighty hands that reach down
to the very marrow of the soul
– that mold and create–
to the hands through which
so great a love is transmitted –
It is to these that it is good to surrender our soul,
above all when we suffer or are afraid.
And in so doing there is a great happiness and great merit.

— Pierre Teilhard de Chardin, SJ.

19th Century: an Immigrant Province
[1831 – 1879]

Although the Society of Jesus was restored world-wide in 1814, Jesuits did not return to the Southern United States until 1831. In the colonial period, Louisiana been a mission of the Paris Provinces but in the return, its parent province was the Lyons Province. The United States was now an independent country, filling with immigrants, and many Know-Nothings who held the immigrants in contempt. The North prospered because of industry and trade, while the South was dedicated to agriculture. If we think of the Brothers who traveled from Europe to the American South as immigrants in their own way, we learn of their countries of origin: Switzerland 31; Germany 28; France 19; Spain 13; Ireland 13; Italy 12, as well as Mexico, Austria, Bohemia, Netherlands, Belgium and Scotland.

For the United States, this century was a time of dynamic growth and development. The country bled during the dreadful Civil War; the emancipation of the Southern slaves resulted in massive dislocation of farm labor. The continent shrank with the expansion of railroads; the mighty Brooklyn Bridge joined the boroughs of New York. Steel, oil and coal fed the rapid development of the growing industrial country.

Br. Joseph Alsberg, SJ
middle 19th century

There are no records about Br. Joseph Alsberg, SJ in the archives of the New Orleans province, probably because he was a member of the Paris province, whose archives are unavailable at this time. The following are two mentions by Michael Kenny, which cover only the first year he was in the New Orleans Mission in 1837.

Failing again with Father Guidée (Jesuit provincial of the Paris province), he (Bishop Antoine Blanc) took his case to the Father General in Rome, and so impressed him that Father Roothaan instructed the French provincial to render the good bishop every possible assistance. Wherefore in December 1836 six Fathers and two Brothers sailed from Le Havre under the leadership of Father Ladavière and reached New Orleans February 22, 1837, the first band of Jesuits to resume their brothers' labors in Lower Louisiana (Kenny, 32).

There (New Orleans) the Bishop entertained them in his episcopal residence with his wonted hospitality, and in a few days they were ready for whatever tasks he should assign them, while awaiting the determination of their college contract. They were: Father Pierre Ladavière, the superior, Father Francis Abbadie and Brother Chauvet, of the Province of Lyons; Fathers Paul Mingard and Joseph Soller and Brother Joseph Alsberg of the province of France (Kenny, 32).

Br. Charles Alsberg, SJ
1789 – 1876

Charles was born in Ooteghem, Belgium on the last day of 1789, and after a long probation was admitted to the Order on October 8, 1827. He served faithfully as tailor and sacristan in various houses of the Society in Belgium until 1836, when he was sent to the New Orleans Mission. There he labored for ten years, after which he was sent to Fordham University, which had come into the hands of Ours shortly before and where he spent the rest of his life. After many years of admirable service, his physical vigor faded away, and he died on March 16, 1876 at the age of 87 (Kenny, 32).

Br. John Aschberger, SJ
1809 – 1858

John was born in Hueb, Bavaria, on December 27, 1809. In 1833 he joined and remained a member of the German province, although he labored most of his life in the American South. The first citation of him is found in the catalogue for 1849, stating that he was assigned to Spring Hill College in Mobile, Ala as a cook, a skill that he used in every community where he subsequently resided. He spent the years 1851-52 at the Jesuit community in Baton Rouge as cook, buyer and dispenser of the common closet. He returned to Spring Hill College for a year, as cook and cabinet maker. He was posted back to Baton Rouge, La for a year in the same capacity, and then back to Spring Hill College, then back to Baton Rouge. He was sent to St. Charles College in Grand Coteau, La with light duties. Finally on January 5, 1858, Br. John Aschberger, SJ died, 48 years old and 25 years a Jesuit.

Br. Edward Kennely, nSJ
1835 – 1861

From his grave stone we learn only this about Edward Kennely, who died as a novice Brother. He was born on January 2, 1835 and died on August 29, 1861.

Br. Andreas Boemecke, SJ
1825 – 1884

Andreas Boemecke was born in Hannover Germany on November 11, 1825. He entered the Society of Jesus at Spring Hill College in Mobile, Ala on June 16, 1850. The fragmentary records we have about Andreas indicate that his signature craft was that of tailor, at which he labored for fifteen years (1870-85). He also served as receptionist and sacristan (1870-85). Br. Andreas Boemecke, SJ died on the fourth of March, 1884, 58 years of age and 34 as a Jesuit Brother.

Br. Charles Boemecke, SJ
1829 – 1899

Charles, brother of Ignatius Boemecke and cousin of Andreas, was also born in Hannover, Germany on October 3, 1829. Like his brother and cousin, he emigrated to the United States to serve in the New Orleans Mission, thus entering the Order in 1850. He was first assigned to the College of the Immaculate Conception in New Orleans where for 15 years he was given the care of the horses and mules of the college; he also served as the buyer for the college, indicating a high degree of literacy. In 1884 he was transferred to Spring Hill College where for five years he performed the same duties (1884-89). In 1897, he was transferred to the infirmary at Grand Coteau, La because of his failing health. On August 17, 1899, Charles Boemecke, SJ died at the age of 71 and 50 as a Jesuit Brother.

Br. Ignatius Boemecke, SJ
1824 – 1912

He was born in Nesselröden, Germany on August 15, 1824, the oldest boy of Ignatius Boemecke and Elisabeth Kaiser. He is, moreover, the brother of Br. Charles Boemecke, SJ and cousin of Br. Andreas Boemecke, SJ. After he was apprenticed to a joiner to learn the carpenter's trade, he set out to travel through Germany, France, Switzerland, and Italy, plying and perfecting his craft. Eventually he arrived in Rome where he had an interview with the Jesuit general, Jan Roothaan. He entered the Society as a brother on June 19, 1847.

He went to France to join a band of volunteers who left Marseilles for New Orleans in 1847, which included Darius Hubert, James Duffo, and many other illustrious pioneers of the New Orleans Mission. Brother Ignatius was sent to the Jesuit church and college in downtown New Orleans, which at that time were just two small frame buildings. There he took his vows in June of 1849 and remained for most of his Jesuit life.

As receptionist he was the face of the Jesuits to the world and the dispenser of charity and advice to the many who came to the door. It is difficult to know how literate this Jesuit Brother was, but Ignatius was assigned to tasks which required a fair grade of literacy. For over fifteen years at the Jesuit College in New Orleans, he served as the assistant procurator, which equivalently means "assistant treasurer"(1880-99). Occasionally he was also the buyer for the house.

There (the schools in New Orleans) for over sixty years, Brother Ignatius was porter, buyer and all-around manager, humble, pious and efficient, loved and prized by the community and people. He was watchful adviser of good Brothers Charles and Andrew, his younger Boemecke brother and cousin. … He had his Diamond Jubilee long before he left his New Orleans post for the first time (Kenny, 158).

Ignatius was the first of thirteen members of his own and extended family who served the New Orleans Mission. One notable thing about the members of this family is their longevity, even in the face of the dreaded yellow fever. They averaged almost fifty years in the Society.

After serving 62 years at Baronne Street, Ignatius Boemecke, SJ was retired to Grand Coteau, La where he occupied his last years in prayers and devotions. He died there on May 29, 1912, three months short of his 88 birthday but 65 years a Jesuit Brother.

Br. Francis Boniface, SJ
1804 – 1864

Francis Boniface was born in Domfront, France on October 28, 1804. We lack information on what he did with his life prior to 1848, when we learn that he was on his way to the New Orleans Mission and life in the Order as a Jesuit Brother. He arrived at Spring Hill College in Mobile, Ala in 1850 and served four years there as the baker. He moved often, first to the college in New Orleans for two years as its baker (1855-56), then back to Spring Hill College for two years as its baker (1857-58), New Orleans for one year and then back to Spring Hill College for four years. His final assignment was to St. Charles College in Grand Coteau, La in 1864. He died on December 11, 1864 at the age of 60 and 16 years a Jesuit Brother.

Br. Emmanuel Brenans, SJ
1797 – 1863

Emmanuel was born in Dournon, Switzerland on March 2, 1797. He joined the Lyons province on March 12, 1826 and was posted to the New Orleans Mission. He spent his first five years at the Jesuit college in New Orleans (1853-59) as the brother who kept the common supplies used by the faculty. The next year he was serving in the same job at Spring Hill College in Mobile, Ala (1858), but he was sent back to New Orleans in 1859. He returned to Spring Hill College where he served out his life performing the same tasks. Emmanuel Brenans, SJ died on February 15, 1863; he was 65 years old and a Jesuit Brother for 37. The following is taken from Michael Kenny, SJ (191): "Spring Hill records her first Brother, Emmanuel Brenans of Lyons, a master of all trades, who from 1847 to 1864 smiled and prayed through every house and farm function and returned from hard labor to receive the last Sacraments and to rest in God."

Br. John Buillard, SJ
1817 – 1852

Our records show that John was a member of the New Orleans Mission of the Lyons province and entered the Order on September 4, 1841. His first assignment was to the Jesuit seminary in Lyons, where he served as tailor, typographer and doorkeeper from 1844-47. After this he crossed the Atlantic and arrived at Spring Hill College in Mobile where he served as cook, tailor and custodian of the students' clothes closet (1848-51). Br. John Buillard died on October 29, 1852, a very young man, a mere 35 years old and only 11 years as a Jesuit Brother. The following except is taken from Kenny (191): "The next Brother (at Spring Hill College) was Brother John Buillard of Friburg, tailor, printer, cook, porter, and what-not, a saintly toiler, and the first Jesuit to find rest in a Spring Hill grave."

Br. Joseph Chauvet, SJ
1804 – 1857

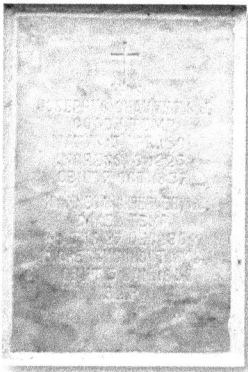

Joseph Chauvet was born in Velleron, France on April 15, 1804 in the middle of Napoleon's successes. When he entered the Lyons province of the Order on August 14, 1825, he was slated for the New Orleans Mission. He arrived in the South in late 1840, and was posted to Spring Hill College in Mobile, Ala for almost all of his Jesuit life. From 1848 to 1854 he served as the buyer for the college and the dispenser of the common supplies. He spent just one year at St. Charles College in Grand Coteau, La (1855) as its buyer and sacristan. Br. Joseph Chauvet died on October 7, 1857; he was a mere 53 years old and a Jesuit Brother for 32 years. Since all information about the Jesuit Brothers is scarce, we include these remarks by Michael Kenny:

Failing again with Father Guide, he (Bishop Antoine Blanc of New Orleans) took his case to the Father General in Rome, who instructed the French provincial to render the good bishop every possible assistance. Wherefore in December 1836 six Fathers and two Brothers sailed from Le Havre under the leadership of Father Ladavière and reached New Orleans February 22, 1837, the first band of Jesuits to resume their brothers' labors in Lower Louisiana (Kenny, 32).

There the Bishop entertained them in his episcopal residence with his wonted hospitality, and in a few days they were ready for whatever tasks he should assign them, while awaiting the determination of their college contract. They were: Father Pierre Ladavière, the superior, Father Francis Abbadie and Brother Chauvet, of the Province of Lyons; Fathers Paul Mingard and Joseph Soller and Brother Joseph Alsberg of the province of France (Kenny 23).

Br. Philip Corné, SJ
1800 – 1862

Philip Corné was born in 1800 in the French town of Doubs. He joined the Lyons province on August 14, 1825 with a view to serving in the New Orleans Mission. After his arrival in the mission, he became the infirmarian of the college in New Orleans (1848), after which he was sent upriver to the new college under way in Baton Rouge. He served as cook, but more importantly, as the buyer for the institution (1850-58). He traveled down river to the college in New Orleans for one year and then returned to Baton Rouge. Br. Philip Corné was 62 years old when he died, and 37 as a Jesuit Brother.

Again, we are indebted to Michael Kenny for further information about Br. Philip:

> Retained at St. Joseph's, Baton Rouge, when the other brothers and all but the pastors were transferred, Brother Corné was the trusty support of Fathers Lavay, Prachensky, Hubert, and Larnaudie. … He is catalogued variously as buyer, baker, farmer, builder, carpenter, but more descriptively *ad omnia*; and for everything in humble and obedient sacrifice, Philip Corné of Lyons was called to his reward at Baton Rouge October 28, 1862 (Kenny 55).

Br. Joseph Ducret, SJ
1807 – 1882

Joseph Ducret was a Savoyard, born on February 15, 1807. Fast forwarding, we know that he emigrated to America to join the New Orleans Mission of the Lyons Province, which he entered on May 24, 1841. His first appearance in the catalogue is at Spring Hill College in Mobile, Ala, where he spent the next thirty-one years of his life. Alternately he was in charge of the distribution of common household items, such as shaving equipment, etc. and he served as a cabinet maker. He became the house manager for the community and occasionally its receptionist. He was in charge of the college students for several years. He later served as the treasurer of the community for four years and as librarian of the college library, both of which skills required literacy. Occasionally, he was in charge of the animals of the college. His tenure at Spring Hill College ended with his last jobs, community buyer and assistant treasurer. Br. Joseph Ducret, SJ died at Spring Hill College on December 18, 1882; he was 75 years old and 41 as a Jesuit Brother.

Joseph Ducret, who left Savoy's army to enter Loyola's in 1841, rendered invaluable service by his skill in various arts and trades and his indefatigable toil. The explosion of a defective cannon that he fired in salute to the Blessed Sacrament at a Corpus Christi Procession blew off his right arm, but he learned to write left-handed and so continued in the treasury office and general direction of Grand Coteau in the Civil War years. He brought in vital provisions through both contending lines; and he resumed service at Spring Hill until in 1882 he passed safe through Heaven's lines forever (Kenny, 192).

Br. Clement Hagan, SJ
1837 – 1885

Clement was born in Valais, Switzerland on September 12, 1837. He joined the New Orleans Mission on February 2, 1861 – hardly an auspicious time to emigrate to the American South. The first assignment we know of after his formation was that of lamp lighter at St. Charles College in Grand Coteau, La (1866). He was sent to the college in New Orleans as cook and overseer of the dining room (1867). He kept moving east to Spring Hill College in Mobile and to the Jesuit residence there, where he served as a general maintenance man (1868-71). He served as refectorian at the college in Grand Coteau (1881-83) and then at the college in New Orleans (1883-84). He is listed as being in Cincinnati for the year 1884-85, and then at Galveston. Br. Clement Hagan, SJ died in Galveston on October 22, 1885, forty-eight years old and twenty-four years a Jesuit Brother.

Br. Patrick Hannon, SJ
1836 – 1886

Patrick Hannon is one more Irishman who, although born in Meath, Ireland in 1836, crossed the ocean to join the New Orleans Mission at the age of forty-six, when he discovered his vocation as a Jesuit Brother. He entered the Society at Florissant, Mo on May 16, 1882, in which Order he was to serve only four years. His first and only assignment was to the college in Grand Coteau, La where he served as tailor from 1883 to 1886. Br. Patrick Hannon, SJ died on December 9, 1886. He was a mere fifty years old and only four years a Jesuit Brother.

Br. Gaspar Heinrichs, SJ
1852 – 1899

Gaspar Heinrichs was born in Aachen, Germany on March 29, 1852. He came to America when he was thirty years old to join the New Orleans Mission and entered the Novitiate at Florissant, Mo on August 31, 1881. After taking vows, he was sent to Spring Hill College in Mobile, Ala for six years, every year taking up new jobs: cook, doorkeeper, keeper of the clothing closet, and lamplighter (1883-

89). He was then sent to the Jesuit residence in Augusta, Ga and he performed the same services as he had in Mobile, with the addition of sacristan (1889-98). Then he was sent to the Jesuit parish in Key West, Fla as cook and sacristan. Br. Gaspar Heinrichs, SJ died there on September 7, 1899. He was young, only forty-eight years old and eighteen as a Jesuit Brother.

Br. Herman Hugh, SJ
1857 – 1882

Herman Hugh was born in Hannover, Germany on August 20, 1857. Not quite twenty-years old, Herman entered the Order at Grand Coteau, La on June 3, 1876. His only assignment was to be assistant cook at the college and that for only one year (1880-81). The next year's assignment was to remain at Grand Coteau to recover from illness. As a very young man just twenty-four years old, Br. Herman Hugh, SJ died on April 24, 1882. He was only six years a Jesuit Brother.

Br. Sebastian (Francis) Imfeld, SJ
1820 – 1886

Francis Imfeld, who was born in Valais, Switzerland on July 6, 1820, originally entered the Lyons Province on February 2, 1861 at the age of forty-one. He served in France for a decade, and was sent to the African Missions of the Lyons province from 1874 to 1877, after which he returned to his province's college in Marseilles. He emigrated to Spring Hill College in Mobile, Ala in 1880 to serve, first as the refectorian there for two years and then as the person in charge of the dining room for four years. It was during this time that, for reasons lost to us, he ceased being called "Sebastian" and was now named "Francis." Br. Francis Imfeld, SJ died at Spring Hill College on November 19, 1886. He was sixty-six years old and twenty-five years a Jesuit Brother.

Br. Charles Jagemann, SJ
1874 – 1897

Charles was born in Hannover, Germany on February 13, 1874. He was merely eighteen years old when he entered the Novitiate in Macon, Ga on September 15, 1892 as a member of the New Orleans Mission. His first and only job was his four-year stay at the college in Grand Coteau, La (1895-97). First he was refectorian and then assigned to the farm. Not only did he enter the Society as a young man, but he died young, on June 8, 1897, a mere twenty-three years old, a Jesuit Brother for only five years.

Br. Joseph Jensch, SJ
1824 – 1873

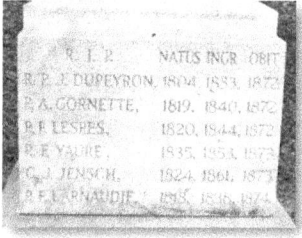

On April 12, 1824 Joseph Jensch was born in Steinhaus, Switzerland. He joined the Lyons province on February 2, 1861 and was eventually sent to its New Orleans Mission. Almost all of his years in the Mission were spent at Spring Hill College in Mobile, Ala, mostly as the college's infirmarian (1866-70). He was then moved to St. Charles College in Grand Coteau, La and labored there for several years. On September 28, 1873 Br. Joseph Jensch, SJ died at Spring Hill College and was buried there. He was forty-nine years old and twelve years a Jesuit Brother. The following is taken from Kenny (191-92):

> Among other Swiss who responded to Father Imsand's appeal was Joseph Jensch, Mayor in Valais, who locked his house, hurled his key into the valley, and never looked back. Steward and manager, he kept Spring Hill's grounds savingly fruitful through the Civil War, and he labored on till in 1873 his faith and toil brought him rest eternal.

Br. Peter Jost, SJ
1842 – 1867

Peter was born on December 8, 1842 in Valais, Switzerland. He is the cousin of Francis Jost, who also became a Jesuit Brother. He joined the Lyons province and eventually labored in the New Orleans Mission. His only posting was to the Immaculate Conception college in New Orleans where he performed many domestic chores. In his seventh year as a Jesuit, he contracted yellow fever and died on October 18, 1867. Br. Peter Jost, SJ was a mere twenty-four years old.

Br. Matthew Kelly, SJ
1839 – 1870

Matthew was born in Kildare, Ireland on April 9, 1837. He joined the Lyons province on June 21, 1859 and was sent to St. Charles College in Grand Coteau, La. He remained there for eight of his eleven years as a Jesuit (1860-1868). The catalogue notes an anomaly, in that he is listed as a novice for four consecutive years. This may be because of ill health. At first he was the gardener charged with food production. He was then posted to Spring Hill College in Mobile, Ala to take care of his fragile health. Br. Matthew Kelly, SJ died on April 17, 1870 at the age of thirty-one and eleven years a Jesuit.

Br. Timothy Kennelly, SJ
1856 – 1879

Timothy was born in Kerry, Ireland on March 27, 1856. He entered the Lyons Province at its Novitiate in Claremont, France on August 11, 1875 as a scholastic novice. The record does not say, but we may conclude that he changed grades while in the Novitiate. He was posted to the tertianship house as refectorian with general house duties. Alas, on January 10. 1879 Br. Timothy Kennelly, SJ died, a mere twenty-two years old and five years a Jesuit brother.

Br. John King, SJ
1822 – 1886

John King was born on July 1, 1822 in Louth, Ireland. When he arrived in America he entered the Missouri vice-province on April 6, 1846. His records are sketchy, but by 1873 he was laboring at the college in Grand Coteau, La, where he spent his entire Jesuit life. From the beginning his major task was that of custodian of the common clothes closet, a task he performed for thirteen years. In addition, he also became for a few years the buyer for the college. Br. John King, SJ died on July 10, 1886, sixty-four years old and forty a Jesuit Brother.

Br. Anthony Kramer, SJ
1809 – 1875

All we know of Anthony Kramer comes from Kenny's history: "Philip Schmidt and Anthony Kramer, big-hearted Wurtemburgers who labored cheerily at all duties into their seventies, won special love and praise, but much the same is said about all those good Brothers. Brother Schmidt was officially house and groundskeeper and horse-and-wagon buyer, and Brother Kramer, cook and watchman, but they did also much else with holy cheer till called to Heaven's joy in 1875 and 1876" (191).

Br. Joseph Kreitzer, SJ
1841 – 1899

Joseph was born in Valais, Switzerland on March 19, 1841. He entered the Novitiate in Macon, Ga on February 2, 1861, just twenty years old. His first assignment was as the cook and baker at Spring Hill College in Mobile, Ala, a task at which he labored for six years (1881-87). He took his culinary skills to the college at Grand Coteau, La where he served for four years, becoming also dispenser of the common closet. Back at Spring Hill College, he served seven more years as cook. He then returned to central Georgia to serve in two Jesuit residences. He spent two years in Augusta, Ga as sacristan, cook, dispenser of the common stock (1887-89), then ten years at the Jesuit residence in Macon, where he continued as cook and sacristan and then maintenance man (1889-99). Br. Joseph Kreitzer, SJ died on July 28, 1899, just shy of sixty years old and thirty-nine as a Jesuit Brother.

Br. Adrian Lagger, SJ
1813 – 1891

Still another man from Valais, Switzerland, Adrian Lagger was born on March 15, 1813. He was nearly fifty years old when he entered the Novitiate of the New Orleans Mission on February 2, 1861. He spent twenty-four years at Spring Hill College in Mobile, Ala as an assistant – assistant cook and assistant receptionist. He was always a maintenance man for the community, as well as the groom of the college's animals. By his seventies, he was no longer capable of heavy lifting. Br. Adrian Lagger, SJ died on January 15, 1891, seventy-eight years old and thirty as a Jesuit Brother.

Br. Michael Maguire, SJ
1835 – 1877

Michael Maguire was born in Dublin, Ireland, on August 23, 1835. He subsequently entered the Lyons province and was sent to the New Orleans Mission. He entered the Order on November 12, 1874. After Novitiate, he lived but one year; Br. Michael Maguire, SJ died on June 27, 1877, fifty-one years old and one year a Jesuit Brother.

Br. Joseph Montegazzi, SJ
1817 – 1892

Joseph Montegazzi was born in Milan, Italy on August 3, 1817. He entered the Jesuit province of Turin on August 4, 1842, and later volunteered for the New Orleans Mission. His only posting was to the Jesuit college in New Orleans where from 1852 to 1893 he served as its cook, infirmarian, buyer and dispenser; this he did almost all of his Jesuit life, namely, the next forty-four years. He was remarkable in that he contacted yellow fever twice and survived both times. On November 28, 1892, Joseph Montegazzi, SJ died at the age of seventy-five and fifty-one years as a Jesuit Brother.

Br. George Müller, SJ
1847 – 1881

George Müller was born in Bavaria, Germany on February 2, 1847. In time he joined the New Orleans Mission on December 8, 1873. He seems to have been a tailor and also the keeper of the common closet. Br. George Müller, SJ died as a very young man on June 6, 1881 at the age of thirty-four years and seven as a Jesuit Brother.

Br. Clement Pfammater, SJ
1810 – 1864

Clement Pfammater was born in Valais, Switzerland on Feb 25, 1810. He entered the German province on October 27, 1833. He first appears in the catalogue of the New Orleans Mission in 1850 when he was assigned to Spring Hill College in Mobile, Ala as receptionist and tailor, tasks he did for three years (1850-53). He served at the college in New Orleans in the same capacity from 1853 until 1864. Br. Clement Pfammater, SJ died on July 12, 1864, fifty-three years old and thirty-one years a Jesuit Brother.

Br. Daniel Rovey, SJ
1801 – 1861

Daniel Rovey was born in Ireland in 1801. He joined the Lyons province and was assigned to the New Orleans Mission. Information about his Jesuit life is not accessible to us, but we have a report on his death and burial at Grand Coteau:

March 1, 1861. Bro Rovey dies this morning shortly after midnight. The body is exposed all day, in his cassock and lying on his bed. Wednesday Ceremonies for the obsequies of Br. Rovey: – office of the dead, low mass, at which the students were not present. Everything according to the custom book (House Diary of St. Charles College).

Br. Daniel Rovey, SJ, was sixty years old when he died. Since we do not know the year he entered the Order, we cannot say how long he was a Jesuit Brother.

Br. Alphonsus Ravy, SJ
1823 – 1867

Alphonsus Ravy was born on April 1, 1823 in Lentiol, France and he entered the Lyons province at Avignon on September 25, 1847. After vows, he remained there for two years as apprentice cook, and spent the next two years in Burgundy as refectorian, cook and gardner (1848-51). He is listed as in transit to the New Orleans Mission in 1853. Upon arrival in 1854, Alphonsus was then posted to Spring Hill College in Mobile, Ala as cook, and then for two years to Baton Rouge, La as baker, refectorian and gardener (1855-57). He moved to St. Charles College in Grand Coteau, La as baker, sacristan and custodian of the wine cellar (1857-67). A mere forty-four years old, Br. Alphonsus Ravy, SJ died on April 2, 1867; he was twenty years a Jesuit Brother.

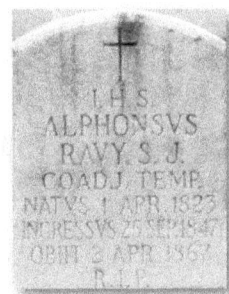

P. P. KENNELY,	1853	1872	1885
P. J. SERRA,	1810	1852	1886
C. F. IMFELD,	1820	1861	1886
S. T. HAGGERTY,	1852	1877	1887
C. J. SAMUEL,	1823	1843	1889
S. M. HUSSEY,	1864	1883	1890
C. C. STAUB,	1811	1839	1891

Br. John Samuel, SJ
1823 – 1889

In Monistrol, France on February 11, 1823 John Samuel was born. Inasmuch as he entered the Novitiate on January 9, 1843, he had to mature quickly, discern a vocation and migrate to America. It appears that he entered the Order with skills in cabinet-making. He is one of the few brothers listed as reader at table, which he did for several years, evidence of considerable literacy. He was sacristan of the college at Grand Coteau, La and at Spring Hill College in Mobile, Ala. His skill in carpentry and cabinet making flowered at Spring Hill College, where he served from 1868 to 1889. His literacy next suited him to be the assistant treasurer at Spring Hill for six year. With clever hands, he also served as the supervisor of the heating system at Spring Hill College for nine years. On November 6, 1889, John Samuel, SJ died at Battles Wharf, Ala. He was sixty-six years of age and forty as a Jesuit Brother.

Br. Simeon Sauzéat, SJ
1824 – 1893

Simeon Sauzéat was born in Ardèche, France on July 22, 1824. He entered the Lyons province of the Society on December 6, 1842, at the age of eighteen. He first appears in the catalogue in 1856 at the College in Grand Coteau, La. For five years he worked there as cabinet maker and carpenter. In addition, he was the buyer for the college for five years and the beadle of the college's students from 1861 to 1891.

Br. Sauzéat became an accomplished smuggler during the Civil War and single-handedly stocked St. Charles College with foodstuffs and tools. "The Brothers supplied meat and cornbread for the farm, and Brother Sauzéat traded wagon loads of cotton in Texas for flour and coffee, and cattle and hogs for salt from the just-discovered New Iberia salt-mines. The Jesuits shared these supplies with their neighbors, and often with the Blue or Gray soldiers, who treated them equally well" (Kenny, 63). "Once Br. Sauzéat and Fr. Robert Kelly were arrested because the latter, an Irish Jesuit at Grand Coteau, had been talking 'too loudly' against the Union who occupied the town. Once the story was told in full, Gen. Butler set free Br. Sauzéat but he visaed the Irish rebel's passage back to Ireland" (Kenny, 63).

Br. Aloysius Schmidt, SJ
1840 – 1899

Aloysius was born in Valais, Switzerland on June 21, 1840. He joined the New Orleans Mission, entering the Order on August 15, 1876. He was assigned to the Jesuit residence in Augusta, Ga as cook, dispenser of common stock, and receptionist, to which was added the duties of sacristan (1880-83). He was moved to the Jesuit residence in Mobile, Ala where for three years he continued the same labors he had done in Augusta (1883-86). He returned to Augusta for one year and then traveled to Macon, Ga and its house of probation, where he labored as cook for four years (1887-91). Although his first task at the college in Galveston was that of cook, he assumed other duties, such as receptionist, dispenser of toiletries, and infirmarian (1891-95). He was posted to the Novitiate in Macon as cook and dispenser (1895-97). Eventually he wound up at the Jesuit college in New Orleans with light duties (1897-99). Br. Aloysius Schmidt, SJ died on August 17, 1899, sixty years old and thirty-eight years a Jesuit Brother.

Br. Philip Schmidt, SJ
1799 – 1876

Philip Schmidt was born in Württemburg, Germany on February 28, 1799. He entered the Order on October 9, 1823. When he was transferred to the New Orleans Mission, he was assigned to Spring Hill College in Mobile, Ala for what appears as the remainder of his Jesuit life. At first he was assigned as general maintenance man for the college. But in 1856 he became the buyer for the college for the rest of his Jesuit life (1856-1876). Evidently he was quite literate when he entered the Order to be entrusted with a task requiring reading, writing and 'rithmatic. Br. Schmidt is reported to have labored cheerily at all duties into his seventies, and won special love and praise. Brother Schmidt was officially groundskeeper and horse-and-wagon buyer. He did also much else with holy cheer until his death on March 29, 1876. He was seventy-seven years old and a Jesuit brother for fifty-three years.

Clockwise from top:

Joseph Strebel
John King
Cornelius Otten
Aloysius Schmidt
Francis Imsand
?? Bellwalter
Joseph Kreitzer
Vincent Blatter
?? Van Gisberger
Simon Sauzéat

Br. Henry M. Schmitz, SJ
1797 – 1843

Henry was born on Jan 2, 1797. He entered the Missouri vice-province and was sent to St. Charles College in Grand Coteau, La during the period when Missouri took over the responsibility for it. He died on Oct 25, 1843 and is buried in the cemetery there.

Br. Anthony Setie, SJ
1815 – 1870

The only information we have about Brother Anthony Setie are the following dates: born November 22, 1815; entered the Order on February 21, 1842; and died on May 13, 1870. Brother Anthony Setie, SJ was fifty-four years old when he died, and a Jesuit Brother for twenty-eight years.

Br. Charles Staub, SJ
1809 – 1854

Charles Staub was born in Zug, Switzerland on October 12, 1809. He joined his brother, Clement, in the German province of the Order. Eventually he was posted to the New Orleans Mission, specifically to the college in Grand Coteau. He served there as miller and baker of the college's grains for five years, which was the rest of his Jesuit life. Br. Charles Staub, SJ died on September 19, 1854, forty-four years old and about twenty as a Jesuit Brother.

Br. Clement Staub, SJ
1811 – 1891

Clement Staub was born in Zug, Switzerland on April 29, 1811. Records show that he entered the German province of the Society of Jesus on June 26, 1841. Clement's right arm was paralyzed, but he traveled to a Marian shrine in Rome and was perfectly cured. Body intact, he was admitted as a Brother with manifold success in many trades. Perhaps he was simply following his brother, Charles, but he traveled to the New Orleans Mission to serve in its institutions, arriving on May 18, 1848. Kenny remarked: "With the aid of Clement Staub and Ignatius Boemecke and other efficient lay brothers, Rev. Hippolyte Gache, first president and pastor of the college of the Immaculate Conception, had the frame buildings (for the college) ready for the opening January 2, 1850" (191). He appears to have been assigned to Spring Hill College and St. Joseph's Church in Mobile, Ala. From 1864 and for many years after he was in charge of the dining room; in 1867 he was designated as the agent of the college in all of its dealings with the city of Mobile, an assignment which required considerable literacy. In 1872 he was transferred to the Jesuit residence attached to St. Joseph's Church in downtown Mobile as sacristan and cook (1872-76). Br. Clement Staub, SJ died on May 20, 1891, eighty years old and fifty years a Jesuit.

Br. Joseph Strebel, SJ
1809 – 1882

Joseph Strebel was born in Aargau, Switzerland on August 12, 1809. He joined the German province on October 30, 1841. Within a few years after his vows, he was sent to the New Orleans Mission. In 1854 he appears for the first time in the catalogue when he is listed as laboring at the college in Grand Coteau, La, where he remained for the rest of his Jesuit life. His range of tasks was indeed varied, for he was briefly a cabinet maker, then a cook, then the person in charge of the wine cellar; he served out of doors as the brother in charge of the college's cattle; all the while he was the college sacristan. As he entered his seventies, his labors were reduced to the light tasks assigned him by the Father Minister. Br. Joseph Strebel, SJ died on December 11, 1882, seventy-three years old and forty-one a Jesuit Brother.

Br. Paul Viboux, SJ
1819 – 1894

Paul Viboux was born in Savoy, Piedmont on March 17, 1819. He came to America as a member of the Lyons province and died a member of that province. Paul entered the Society of Jesus on August 15, 1838. Ten years later we learn that he was en route to the New Orleans Mission to put down roots at the college in Grand Coteau, La in 1851, where remained for many years. When he was posted to Spring Hill College in Mobile, Ala, he was assigned as the house manager, as well as keeper of the clothes closet. He was moved back to the college in Grand Coteau where for six years he continued to be the keeper of the clothing closet; for two years he served as the buyer for the community (1886-94). His failing health forced him to relinquish his duties. Paul Viboux, SJ died on June 28, 1894; he was seventy-five years old and a Jesuit Brother for fifty-six years.

Br. Henry Visconti, SJ
1793 – 1853

"On October 7, 1853, Brother Henry Visconti, a qualified physician from Milan who had spent twenty-seven of his sixty years in the Society, mostly as infirmarian, and had been giving his skilled services to the sick (yellow fever victims), with equal generosity shared joyously in the same reward" (Kenny, 54).

The New Mexico - Denver Mission
[1867 – 1919]

An important development began in the western states of America, in the lands taken from Mexico in the mid-19th century. Although we are focusing on the Brothers of the New Orleans Mission and Province, another mission to the West was begun by a group of Jesuits from the Naples Province. That province was suppressed for political reasons, which meant that many brothers and priests were idle and available. Bishop John Baptist Lamy (of *Death Comes to the Archbishop* fame) traveled to Rome to request Jesuits for his missionary projects in New Mexico and Colorado. He was successful, for in August 1867 five Jesuits arrived in Santa Fe from Leavenworth, Kan, along with three Sisters of Loretto, two Sisters of Charity of Cincinnati, and two Brothers of the Christian Schools. The Bishop wrote to "Very Reverend and Dear Father Sopranis (Visitor in charge of the American provinces): "Fathers Gasparri and Bianchi with Brother Vezza arrived here on the first of May. Please thank your most reverend Father General" (May 6, 1868 in Steele, *Works and Days*, 3) Among the Jesuit group there were two priests and two brothers, Prisco Caso and Raphael Vezza. Stansell describes the arrival of this group in Santa Fe: "Four of the five Jesuits were newcomers to the United States. … two were lay brothers and two were priests. One of the Brothers, Prisco Caso, had been in Naples at the time he received his assignment as cook; as such, he was to prove himself indispensable to the well-being of his companions. The other Brother, Raphael Vezza, was a carpenter. In 1871 two of these Brothers remained in Albuquerque, Luigi Grimaldi, tailor and Raffaele Acampora, cook."

Thomas Steele SJ, writing about the Jesuits in Albuquerque in 1871-1872, said: "In August 1871, further reinforcement of four men arrived, Fr. Salvatore Personè, Carlo's younger brother, and three lay brothers. … At this time there were two scholastic novices, young men preparing to study for the priesthood, and five novice brothers, who in these years often without education, even the ability to read and write. … On 21 April 1882, Novice Brother Florentino Romero, from Agua Fria outside of Santa Fe and Conejos, died in the Novitiate of erisipelas at the age of nineteen" (Steele, *Works and Days*, 41-42).

Steele records the folly of the brothers petitioning to wear the heavy ankle-length cassock, as the scholastics did. Be careful what you ask for: "During June of 1888, Jesuit headquarters decreed that the Jesuit Brothers might wear the black cassock, just as the priests and scholastics did. The Brothers had agitated for cassocks quite a few years before, and when the scholastic novices in the short-lived Albuquerque Novitiate wore them, the Brothers in vows had again complained briefly before resigning themselves to patience. Ten years later Rome got around to acting, and the Brothers had the pleasure of discovering for the first time on 15 August how comfortable a floor-length (black) wrapper of stiff wool can be on a hot summer's day" (Steele, *Works and Days*, 44).

Jesuits of the Naples province arrived on a permanent basis in El Paso, Tex on October 14, 1881, and they assumed care of a string of neglected 200-year-old missions. They went on to establish and maintain more than 30 parishes. The next generation of Neopolitan Jesuits was led by Fr. Pinto, SJ who himself built 14 churches and 7 schools. Our records are incomplete, so we cannot say how many Brothers worked in El Paso or what tasks they performed. But in 1919 when El Paso came under the jurisdiction of the New Orleans province, there were 185 Jesuits working in the area. Several of these are identified by means of the gravestones in Concordia Cemetery, but the anonymity of the rest reinforces a remark made earlier about the "nameless" brothers.

This Mission of the Naples province steadily grew: in 1867 = 5; 1881 = 15; 1877 = 35; 1879 = 50 and 1919 = 85. The works undertaken by these men extended in two directions: Albuquerque and environs and Colorado. It is the labors of the Jesuit Brothers working in New Mexico and West Texas that we focus on. The tradition of the Society was to work in schools, not parishes. The attempted college in Albuquerque failed, but the building of a college in Las Vegas succeeded. The Jesuits took responsibility for San Felipe Neri parish in Old Town, Albuquerque, and founded other satellite churches to the south and west of the city. Every one of these churches or missions required Brothers to provide the essential services to maintain the ministry.

Until the New Mexico - Colorado Mission ended in 1919, all records of the Jesuits working there were kept by the Naples Province, which materials are not readably accessible to us now. Yet we have two sources for information to sketch the lives of these men and to provide basic information. There are two Jesuit cemeteries, one in Albuquerque and another in El Paso, in which the Brothers of the Naples province were interred. We have also the occasional obituary from the Naples province, some House Journals, and the narratives constructed by Harold Stansell and Thomas Steele. We record only the graves of the Jesuit Brothers buried in these two cemeteries.

Jesuit graves in Santa Barbara Cemetery, Albuquerque, NM	Jesuit graves in Concordia Cemetery, El Paso, TX
C. Florintinus Romero, nSJ 16 Oct 1862 – 21 Apr 1882	Br. Manuel Ugarte, SJ 30 Dec 1851 – 4 Jan 1904
C. Paschalis Pandolfi, SJ 24 Feb 1831 – 26 Feb 1905	Br. Anthony Gros, SJ 12 Dec 1847 – 22 Nov 1917
C. Jacobus McGlennon, SJ 15 Dec 1850 – 25 May 1909	Br. Fabian Soto, SJ 20 Jan 1864 – 5 Feb 1920
C. Aloisius Talamo, SJ 7 Apr 1830 – 2 Sept 1914	
C. Landolphus Zavorati, SJ 2 Sept 1869 – 1 July 1924	
C. Josephus Quaranta, SJ 19 Mar 1832 – 22 Mar 1926	
C. Cherubin Ansalone, SJ 27 Apr 1830 – 28 Sept 1908	
C. Immanuel Celaya, SJ 8 May 1862 – 14 Mar 1909	
C. Caietanus Veniero, SJ 15 Aug 1823 – 3 Nov 1909	
C. Michael Cofano, SJ 1 Jan 1827 – 13 Jan 1912	

The format for this section of the book differs from the others. There the Brothers are listed alphabetically and by time period. But here, in an attempt to tell as much of the story of the Neapolitan brothers in the West as is possible, it seems better to treat them chronologically. The story of these men is quite unknown to most Jesuits, even members of the New Orleans province, so an historical format has much to recommend itself.

The Jesuit Community in Albuquerque in 1872

We quote this record of the status of the Jesuit community in Albuquerque in 1872, first because it describes the growth of Jesuits in the area from five in 1867 to nine in 1872. Moreover, in the list of five Brothers, we have brief mention of two for whom we have no other information.

In 1872, the status of the Albuquerque House included:

Fr. Donato Gasparri	– Superior, Business Manager, parish priest
Fr. Carlo Personè	– Pastor, Spiritual Father, Consultor, parish priest
Fr. Alessandro Leone	– Schoolmaster, Minister, Consultor, parish priest
Fr. Pasquale Tomassini	– taking care of the Socorro parish
Br. Raffaele Acampora	– Cook, Excitator, Visitor at meditation and examination
Br. Luigi Grimaldi	– Tailor, Sacristan
Br. Michael Cofano	– Carpenter
Br. Pasquale Pandolfi	– Gardener
Br. Prisco Caso	– in Socorro, general worker

(Steele, *Works and Days*, 123-128).

Only by chance do we know anything about Raffaele Acampora, the cook, and Luigi Grimaldi, the tailor and sacristan. But we note that the fathers were listed first, and the brothers next.

Br. Gaetano Muscat, SJ
???? – 1871

Brother Gaetano Muscat, a Maltese, arrived in the community to replace Brother Vezza. "On 30 March, Brother Vezza, who already had permission to leave from Fr. Provincial, set out for Woodstock, Maryland. Brother Gaetano Muscat took his place and his job, arriving 10 May" (Steele, *Works and Days*, 35). He is listed in the status, an annual list of assignments, of the house in Albuquerque as "carpenter, general worker." The record of a dying Brother is indeed rare, and so we cite this one in full:

> We gave the last sacraments to Brother Muscat this morning. At noon Brother Muscat surrendered his spirit to his Creator while breathing lightly. Many people came to view the body. The next day (Wednesday of Holy Week) there was a modest funeral. Fr. Superior Gasparri sang the mass and preached briefly about the life of the deceased Brother, then the fathers read the office beside the coffin. We wanted the burial to be fitting, for the edification of the people, since he was the first Jesuit to die in this plaza. The son of Lucero, the schoolmaster, who had been a disciple of the dead brother for some months, bore the corpse to the grave site out of a room on the left side of the small door of the church. They cried a great deal at the moment for lowering the body, because of the special circumstances. (Steele, *Works and Days*, 40).

Br. Florentinus Romero, nSJ
1862 – 1882

Mention of his arrival in the Southwest was made earlier. We note here only his life, which was very brief: "On 21 April 1882, Novice Brother Florentinus Romero, from Agua Fria outside of Santa Fe and Conejos, died in the Novitiate of erisipelas at the age of nineteen" (Steele, 42). Florentinus died still a novice in Albuquerque, NM and was buried in Santa Barbara Cemetery. He was twenty years old" (Steele, 41-42).

Br. Prisco Caso, SJ
1825 – 1886

On August 15, 1867, five Jesuits, members of the dispersed province of Naples, arrived in Santa Fe. They had traveled in a caravan that left Leavenworth, Kan, on June 14 in the company of Jean Baptiste Lamy, Bishop of Santa Fe. They came to minister to the religious needs of the Spanish-speaking people and eventually to found an institution of higher learning which was to serve the needs of the Catholic Church in the Rocky Mountain Region.

Only fragmentary bits of information about Br. Caso survive, such as his posting to Socorro, NM in 1871 as "general worker" (Stansell, *Regis: the Crest of the West* 1-2). Prisco was a member of the Naples province, born in Naples on February 28, 1825. His band of travelers is famous for having escaped an attack of Indians. While accompanying Fr. Tomassini in an expedition to Socorro, this man of many adventures was nearly drowned in the Rio Grande. Later stationed at Conejos, he had to face the inclemency of two winters, destitute of almost any means but his tried patience. In another poor and solitary residence he even endured the pains of starvation, and what is at times still worse, the gloominess of perfect seclusion, especially when Fr. Carrozzini, his Superior, went out on missionary excursions. He died unexpectedly in Ysleta on September 8, 1886.

Br. Patrick Wallace, SJ
no dates available

We know that Patrick was of Irish extraction, although we do not know when or where he entered the Order, much less how he found his way to the Jesuit College in Las Vegas, NM. Three times Stansell tells us that Patrick Wallace's ministry pointed inward in service of his fellow Jesuits and outward as a teacher of the preparatory class in the college (35). In another place Stansell says of Patrick that he was the "prefect of Health and teacher of third class of English" (27). Stansell's book mainly focuses on the building of Jesuit schools, and so he would favor mentioning lay brothers who could teach.

Br. Raphael Vezza, SJ
1826 – 1889

Raphael was born in Naples on Oct 24, 1826 and entered the Order on April 11, 1850. Raphael was directed to St. Mary's College in Montreal, where he took his vows in August 1865. A year later he was assigned as companion to Fr. D. Vitale, who had become insane and was obliged to go to Barcelona. Shortly after, the Neapolitan fathers decided to begin a mission in New Mexico, which is why we find him next in the American Southwest.

On August 15, 1867, five Jesuits, members of the dispersed province of Naples, arrived in Santa Fe. Brother Prisco Caso, who had been in Naples at the time he received his assignment, was a cook, an indispensable job for the well-being of his companions. The other Brother, Raphael Vezza, was a carpenter, who employed his skill to construct various buildings. He worked two years on a church which was destroyed by a violent earthquake, which flattened the church and college there. Brother Vezza was later posted to Woodstock, Md as a master carpenter to help build the Jesuit college there. After a life of service, Br. Vezza SJ died in Maryland and was buried there.

Br. Emmanuel Ugarte, SJ
1851 – 1904

In her book on Carlos Pinto, SJ, Sister Owen records from the house journal of the Jesuit community in Ysleta two very brief comments. She notes that Br. Ugarte left with Fr. Penella to go to the Ysleta community (Dec 31, 1890) and that he belonged to the community which arose after the closing of Ysleta. The only other information we have on Br. Ugarte comes from his gravestone, namely, he was fifty-three years old when he died and twenty-six years a Jesuit.

(born)   December 30, 1851
(entered) March 17, 1878
(died)   January 3, 1904
        El Paso, TX

Br. Paschal Pandolfi, SJ
1824 – 1905

Paschal was born in Naples, Italy on June 11, 1824. He entered the Order on September 20, 1854, at the age of twenty-three. He was trained as a cook and spent some time in that capacity in Naples. In 1860 he was sent to the *Collegium Nobilium* in Rome as cook, but later to the *Collegium Germanicum* where he assumed a new and important task, namely, buyer. In 1875, he was sent to the New Mexico Mission in Albuquerque as its gardener and food producer, a job he fulfilled excellently for his whole life.

In 1900 he was devastated with "severe and most painful gallstones" and despite seeking medical help in Trinidad, Las Vegas and Albuquerque, he found no relief. When he suffered a re-occurrence of this in early 1905, a physician in Albuquerque recommended surgery "with the maximum probability of being restored to health." Paschal was now seventy-three years old and had just celebrated his jubilee of being fifty years a Jesuit. So he underwent surgery on February 15, 1905; the surgeon removed seven gallstones of exceptional weight, "as large as nuts." Paschal recovered well for a week or so, but was stricken with a fever and it was evident that his life was about to end. His community brought him Viaticum and he was given the Last Rites. On February 27, 1905, Br. Paschal Pandolfi, SJ died. His funeral rites were done at San Felipe Neri, the Jesuit church in Old Town, and he was buried in the cemetery of St. Barbara in Albuquerque. He was eighty years old and fifty-one years a Jesuit Brother.

Br. Cherubin Ansalone, SJ
1830 – 1908

Cherubin was born in Salerno, a suburb of Naples, Italy, on April 27, 1830. Almost thirty years later he entered the Society on October 27, 1859. When the province was suppressed by the Italian government and its members dispersed, Cherubin returned to his family, but continued to be listed among the members of the province. With no explanation available to us, he traveled to the American West. As of September 1869, he was listed as a member of the New Mexico Jesuits among whom he became a Brother, taking vows on February 2, 1880. He did many jobs and did them well: tailor, cook, receptionist, custodian of the common closet, and sacristan of exceptional piety. He was skilled at adorning the altar in its various seasonal attire. He constructed there a crèche of Neopolitan quality. He was for his brethren a model of Jesuit piety. For two years Br. Cherubin suffered from acute stomach disease, dying on September 28, 1908 in Albuquerque; he was 78 years old and 49 years a Jesuit Brother.

Br. Giovanni Tateo, SJ
exact dates unknown

This comment by Thomas Steele (*Works and Days*, 128) is the only mention we have of Br. Tateo:

> The house had scarcely been gotten ready to be lived in when more fathers and brothers arrived from Europe. These were Frs. Lorenzo Fede, Enrico Ferrari, Carlo Pinto and Vito Tromby and Bros. Giovanni Tateo and Gaetano Veniero. They left Naples on 1 May and arrived in Albuquerque on the nones (5th) of June (approximate date: 1875).

Br. Emmanuel Celaya, SJ
1862 – 1909

Emmanuel Celaya was born in Mexico on May 8, 1862. He has the distinction of entering the Society on June 21, 1879, just after his seventeenth birthday. At that time, there was a House of Probation in Albuquerque, where he trained as a tailor. He was so adept at this, that he continued this craft for the rest of his Jesuit life. His health declined, with labored breathing. It was thought that the air at the college in Las Vegas, NM would benefit him. But on March 14, 1909, Br. Emmanuel Celaya, SJ died, a mere 46 years old and 30 as a Jesuit Brother.

Common Grave Stone of Early Jesuits Buried in Albuquerque, NM

Br. Cajetan Veniero, SJ
1823 – 1909

Cajetan Veniero was born in Naples on August 23, 1823. The most noteworthy event in his youth was the fact that he would inherit "many thousands of dollars," which ultimately he donated to the Society. He finally entered the Order on March 18, 1852. He too suffered the severe dislocation of the suppression of the Neapolitan Jesuits and was internally exiled in the area for over ten years. Finally, a Jesuit house was established and Cajetan "returned home" to Italy in 1870. Just three years later, in 1873, he was sent to the New Mexico Mission, where for thirty years he served as tailor, sacristan, custodian of the community clothes closet and launderer. Eventually he became deaf and his eyesight failed; nevertheless he attended to his own hygiene and cleanliness, so as not to impose any burden on his fellow Jesuits. On November 3, 1909 Br. Cajetan Veniero, SJ died in Albuquerque and was buried there; he was eighty-six years old and a Jesuit Brother for fifty-seven.

Br. James McGlennon, SJ
1846 – 1909

The only information we have on this brother is that recorded on his gravestone in the Cemetery of St. Barbara in Albuquerque. From it we deduce that he was fifty years old when he died and a Jesuit brother for ten years.

(born)   December 15, 1859
(entered) October 30, 1899
(died)   May 15, 1909
Albuquerque.

Br. Michael Cofano, SJ
1827 – 1912

Michael Cofano was born in Foggia, Italy on January 1, 1827. We know that he entered the Novitiate of the Naples Province and was part of the wave of Neapolitan Jesuits who migrated to the New Mexico Mission in the late 1800s. It appears that he spent the rest of his life in and around Albuquerque, where the Society staffed many parishes. He was an exceptional carpenter, who built two roulette tables for the men of Albuquerque (his superior was absent then). Later he enlarged the niche over the main altar to hold a new and larger statue of St. Ignatius. "On 9 June Brother Cofano, who had returned from Las Vagas, finished the two new confessionals." (Steele, 72)

Because of its unusual character, we include the very rare mention of the final vows of a Jesuit Brother: "… toward the end of November, Fr. Salvatore Personè and Brother Michael Cofano took their last vows" (Stansell, 60). Br. Michael Cofano, SJ died in Albuquerque on January 13, 1912; he was 85 years old and approximately 60 as a Jesuit Brother.

Br. Luigi Talamo, SJ
1830 – 1914

Luigi was born on April 7, 1830 in the southern Italian town of Sorrento. Twenty-one years later, on April 21, 1851, he joined the Naples Province as a Jesuit Brother. He labored in the Naples province until it was suppressed and its members dispersed. When the bishops of the western United States appealed to Father General for assistance in the Mission, many Jesuits of the Naples province were recruited to the American West — priests and, of course, Brothers, who ran the institutions. He labored in the New Mexico Mission for forty years, always as a cobbler. On September 2, 1914 Br. Luigi Talamo, SJ died in Albuquerque; he was eighty-five years old and sixty-four as a Jesuit Brother.

Br. Antonio Gros, SJ
1847 – 1917

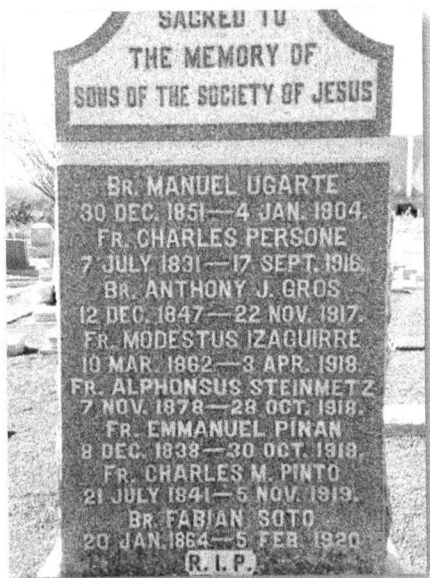

Antonio, a native of Barcelona, Spain, was born on December 12, 1847. He entered the Aragon Province on August 14, 1874. Shortly after, he embarked for "the New Mexico/ Colorado Mission," where he labored for the rest of his life. Little is recorded of his life except that he took his final vows on August 15, 1884. Like most brothers on the frontier, he was adept at many jobs. His death notice in the Naples Province records describes him as pious and a lover of labor. On November 22, 1917 Br. Antonio Gros, SJ died: he was seventy-eight years old and forty-three a Jesuit brother. He is buried in El Paso in the Jesuit section of Concordia Cemetery.

The End of the New Mexico/Denver Mission: 1919

In 1919 the Vatican no longer considered the work of the Jesuits in the Southwest as a "Mission," since the Catholics there were now numerous and the Jesuits of the United States were sufficient to serve them. Because New Mexico and Colorado were no longer a canonical mission of the Naples province, its territory and the Jesuits working there were put in the charge of the two American provinces who were already serving there, Missouri and New Orleans. Missouri assumed care of Colorado, and New Orleans of New Mexico and West Texas. Most of the Jesuits working there were members of the Naples province, whose "mission" just ended. They were given the choice to remain where they were working and so become part of the province which assumed care of it or to return to Naples. This choice determined the remaining apostolic work of the Brothers laboring there.

Br. Fabian Soto, SJ
1864 – 1920

Fabian was born in Burgos, Spain on January 20, 1864. Somewhere along the way, he came to North America and joined the Mexican province on January 16, 1901. Thereafter he labored in both El Paso, Texas and Albuquerque in the New Mexico Mission. There are no records about where he worked or the labors he performed. Brother Fabian Soto SJ died in El Paso on February 5, 1920 and was buried in the Jesuit plot of the Concordia Cemetery in El Paso. He was fifty-six years old and nineteen years a Jesuit.

Br. Landulphus Zavorati, SJ
1869 – 1924

Landulphus Zavorati, born in Padua, Italy on Sept 2, 1869, entered the Order on August 15, 1899. Along with many other Italian Jesuits who were harassed by the government, he was sent to the New Mexico / Denver Mission. Given the choice in 1919 of remaining in the West or returning to Naples, Landulphus Zavorati opted to remain and was then posted to El Paso, Texas as a maintenance man (1919-22). He then became the receptionist and sacristan for the Jesuit Church for two years (1922-24). Br. Landulphus Zavorati, SJ remained in El Paso until his death on July 1, 1924; he was fifty-five years old and a Jesuit Brother for twenty-five years.

Br. Joseph Quaranta, SJ
1882 – 1926

Joseph Quaranta was born in Grottaglie, Italy on March 19, 1882. He followed his brother, Francis Quaranta, into the Order, and entered the Novitiate on December 4, 1904. He served in the New Mexico Mission until 1919, when the territory was put in the charge of the New Orleans province. Up until then we have no record of his work, probably because he remained a member of the Naples province and was listed in their catalogue. The New Orleans catalogues record that in 1919 he was serving at San Felipe Church in Old Town, Albuquerque. It would seem that he labored all of his Jesuit life before 1919 also in Albuquerque. Moreover, his sole job there was that of receptionist for the parish and the Jesuit residence. Br. Joseph Quaranta, SJ died on March 22, 1926; he was only forty-four years old and twenty-four a Jesuit Brother.

Br. Valentine Lopez, SJ
1860 – 1928

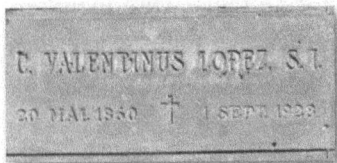

Valentine Lopez was a native of New Mexico, who was born in Santa Fe on May 20, 1860 and entered the Order on September 1, 1882. He was to spend his entire Jesuit life in New Mexico's "2nd city," Albuquerque. Our records indicate that he labored at San Felipe Neri Parish for nine years (1919-28). He was first and foremost the community's cook and he also cultivated a garden which produced the food for the community's table. He had another job as dispenser of common items to the community. Br. Valentine Lopez, SJ died in Albuquerque on September 1, 1928 and was buried in the Jesuit cemetery there. He was sixty-eight years old and forty-six a Jesuit Brother.

Br. Angelo Urrutia, SJ
1856 – 1933

Angelo Urrutia was born on March 3, 1856 in Guipúzcoa, Spain, in the Basque homeland of St. Ignatius. Upon arrival in America, he entered the Novitiate in Macon, Ga on January 15, 1880. He was, of course, a native Spanish speaker, and so he was sent to the missions in the west. He was in Albuquerque when the New Mexico / Denver Mission was dissolved, thus he was given the choice either to return to his Spanish province or remain, in this case, in New Mexico, now part of the New Orleans Province. As of 1919, he is listed as serving as refectorian and infirmarian at San Felipe in Albuquerque. Occasionally he was asked to be the sacristan of the parish and as the cultivator of its produce garden. He served there from 1919 until 1933. Br. Angelo Urrutia, SJ died on February 20, 1933, seventy-six years old and fifty-three as a Jesuit Brother.

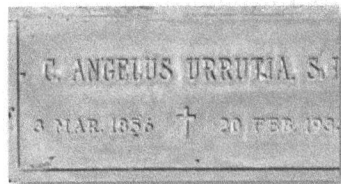

Br. John Martinez, SJ
1878 – 1944

John Martinez was born in Naples, Italy on February 15, 1878. He eventually traveled to the Southwest USA, to work in the New Mexico / Denver Mission. When the Mission was dissolved in 1919, Brother John Martinez chose to return home to Naples, to live the rest of his life as a Jesuit Brother. He is listed as performing in Naples the same services he provided in the Southwest, namely, assistance to the aged and infirm (1919-39). Toward the end of his life the wine cellar was put in his care. Br. John Martinez, SJ died in Naples on May 1, 1944 at the age of sixty-six and forty-seven a Jesuit Brother.

Br. Benjamin Tovani, SJ
no dates available

We have little detail of the Jesuit life of Br. Benjamin Tovani, SJ. He appears in the narrative about the time that the New Mexico - Colorado Mission was dissolved., as a stalwart of Regis College in Denver. We know that his major service was that of infirmarian for sixty-five years.

Br. Anthony Uliano, SJ.
1884 – 1965

Most people who knew him called him "Brother Julian." Born on January 13, 1884, he entered the Society on March 18, 1901 and was assigned to Regis College in Denver in 1906. When Colorado became part of the Missouri Province, he served at Regis College as porter and tailor for sixty years until his death in 1965. Br. Anthony Uliano, SJ died on November 21, 1965; he was eighty-one years old and a Jesuit Brother for sixty-four years.

Br. Joseph Dominguez, SJ
no dates available

It appears that Joseph Dominguez joined the Jesuit staff of the college in Morrison, CO at its inception. He was, to the delight of many, the cook. This is all we know of him.

The Independent Mission
and the Province of New Orleans
[1880 – 1930]

The Society of Jesus was restored in the Church in 1814 and by 1831 the New Orleans Mission was staffed by members of the Paris Province. In April of 1847, the US South became a "Mission of the Lyons Province," when the governance of the Mission was handed over to the Lyons Province and remained so for fifty years. The population of the Lyons mission increased and the foundations of a stable ministry developed to such a degree that the entity known as the "Mission of New Orleans of the Lyons Province" became the "Independent Mission of New Orleans" in 1880, with all ties to Lyons cut. The number of Jesuits in the Independent Mission in 1880 was 135 and by 1930, it had risen to 340. The apostolic works of the Mission consisted of 8 colleges, high schools, parishes, and a mission band. By 1930, the colleges had decreased to 2 and were included with high schools old and new, many new parishes, and a retreat house, which numbered 18 apostolic residences. By far the two ministries in which the Order invested its men were education and parochial service.

The United States fought a war with Spain, acquiring the Philippines and Puerto Rico. Then in 1914, the Great War began, into which the United States was eventually drawn. No sooner had that squandering of life ended, then the Great Flu swept through countries world wide. It created chaos for most cities and towns in the United State. For example, six months in 1918 saw the population of Selma, Ala where Jesuits served as parish priests, quarantined: no one entering there and no one leaving. Great migrations of Europeans and Asians continued to sweep over the States, filling in the remaining agricultural land and providing the work force for a mighty industrial machine. The Catholic population of the States was growing, but concentrated on the East Coast and in cities that attracted Irish, Italian and German immigrants.

But one particular difficulty arose early in the history of the Lyons Mission, as it was morphing into the Independent Mission: language and culture. As early as 1844, the Provincial wrote to the Mission of New Orleans this exhortation:

> Let all endeavor and make flourish union and fraternal charity in all things. Let them ban from recreations all political discussions and all words that contain a nationalistic spirit. We should be on our guard never to permit any remark that rebounds against the nationality of anyone whatsoever, except when there is good to say about it. The nationalistic (*sic*) is the bane of religious houses, is the cause of many dissensions, and of a great number of evils and sins. We are no longer either Irish, or Belgians, or French, or German, etc.; we are Jesuits, members of the same community and brothers of Jesus Christ" (House Diary of St. Charles College, July 14, 1844, translated from the French by George St. Paul, SJ).

These remarks were founded on complaints made to Very Rev. Fr. General and passed on to Father Provincial. The diary of Conrad Widman, SJ contains an estimate of nationalities from 1837 to 1894: "Irish, one hundred and thirty-five; German and German Swiss, one hundred and twenty-six; Americans, one hundred and ten; French and French Swiss, ninety-four; Spanish, twenty; English, nineteen; Italians, nine" (Kenny, 125). The problems with language showed themselves in the way the new generation of English-speaking Jesuits became polarized. Recent entrants into the Society found French ways and language irksome and were outspoken claimants for American government in American fashion. "French," "Irish," "German," "Alsatian," and "American," etc. began to be heard with the implication that promotion and advancement were sometimes conditioned less by merit than by origin. Since the majority of the Brothers of the late 1800's had come from continental Europe, we would imagine that their world would be polyglot, with some of this partisanship.

Br. Andrew Albert, SJ
1832 – 1891

Andrew Albert was born in the Catholic Rhineland, Urspringen, Germany, on January 17, 1832. He immigrated to the United States in October of 1855 to join the New Orleans Mission and entered the Novitiate on Oct 8, 1855. His first assignment was to St. Charles College in Grand Coteau, La as infirmarian and tailor. After a year he was posted to Spring Hill College in Mobile, Ala (1860), but the following year he was assigned to the College of the Immaculate Conception in New Orleans where he spent a decade as its sacristan. In 1871, he was transferred to Spring Hill College primarily as its sacristan (1871-78), but with other tasks assigned. Br. Andrew Albert, SJ died at the Novitiate of St. Stanislaus in Macon, Ga on June 4, 1891; he was 59 years old and 36 years a Jesuit Brother.

R. I. P.	NATUS	INGR	OBIT
P. L. NICOLET,	1864,	1882,	1901
S. G. REILLY,	1877,	1893,	1901
P. B. MAGUIRE,	1849,	1878,	1901
C. P. MORGE,	1846,	1866,	1902
S. J. CLEMENTS,	1877,	1892,	1903
S. M. McCARTHY,	1874,	1892,	1903
R. J. HEIDENKAMP,	1829,	1871,	1903
G. A. ALBERT,	1829,	1854,	1904

Br. Anthony Albert, SJ
1829 – 1904

Anthony is the blood brother of Andrew Albert, and his Jesuit brother in the same New Orleans Mission. On August 15, 1868, he entered the Society, and made his Novitiate at Spring Hill College in Mobile, Ala. He spent the first part of his Jesuit life at Spring Hill, assigned as baker and as groom to the college's horses and mules (1880-84). He was transferred to the Jesuit College in Galveston, Texas where he served as cook and the purveyor of the common supplies for the Jesuit community (1885-87). He was then moved to Macon, Ga, where he continued to perform the same services, as well as helping with the construction of the new St. Joseph church (1887-91). At the age of 74 and 36 years as a Jesuit Brother, Anthony Albert, SJ died on July 18, 1904.

Br. Francis Amacher, SJ.
1847 – 1917

Francis Amacher was born in Eischol, Switzerland on September 20, 1847. He traveled to America to join the New Orleans Mission, and arrived in Grand Coteau, La on September 13, 1873. Records for the next seven years are not available, but with the establishment of the Independent New Orleans Mission, we finally have complete information. His first five years were spent at Spring Hill College in Mobile, Ala as infirmarian and as brother-for-all needs (1880-85). After two years at the college in New Orleans as infirmarian and porter (1886-87), he spent two years in Selma, Ala as cook, sacristan, porter and dispenser of common items (1888-89). Then he returned to New Orleans for ten years as infirmarian, as well as porter and assistant librarian (1890-99). He returned to Spring Hill for three years as infirmarian, sacristan and custodian of the wine cellar (1900-02). Francis was sent to the college in Grand Coteau for three years as porter, sacristan and lamplighter (1903-05). He served at the College of the Sacred Heart in Augusta, Ga as sacristan, infirmarian, porter and clothes custodian (1906-07). He returned to Spring Hill College with reduced duties, namely, assistant infirmarian (1908-14) and back to New Orleans for two years. Finally in 1917, this well-traveled Jesuit Brother, Francis Amacher, SJ, was retired to the infirmary in Grand Coteau where he died on May 21, 1917, 69 years old and 44 years a Jesuit Brother.

Br. John Birmingham, SJ
1864 – 1932

John Birmingham was born in Listowel, Ireland, on February 2, 1864. It is likely that he was intent on joining the New Orleans Mission when he emigrated to the States and entered the Society on July 3, 1896. After his formation, he went to the Jesuit Residence in Augusta, Ga as porter, sacristan and maintenance man. After a year at Spring Hill in Mobile, Ala, where he served as refectorian (1902-03), he was posted to the college in Galveston, Texas for six years (1903-08) basically performing the same service he had been doing, with the addition of caretaker of the wine cellar. He went to Loyola in New Orleans to serve as assistant infirmarian (1908-10). John took these new skills back to Galveston to add to his service of refectorian, doorkeeper and keeper of

the common closet (1910-16). He returned to Loyola for eight years wearing the same hats as he did in Galveston (1917-25). After two years at Spring Hill (1925-27), he returned to New Orleans, this time to Jesuit High School for three years (1927-30). Finally he was assigned to Hot Springs, NC to perform his usual tasks (1930-32). But John was becoming feeble and so was sent to the province infirmary at Grand Coteau, La. Br. John Birmingham, SJ died on August 10, 1932; he was 68 years old and a Jesuit Brother for 36 years.

Br. Richard J. Black, SJ
1869 – 1947

Richard J. Black was born in Glasgow, Scotland on November 29, 1869. We know nothing about his emigration to America or his life until he entered the Order at Florissant, Mo on June 13, 1884. His first assignment was to serve as cook at Jesuit High in New Orleans (1885-86). Soon his culinary skill was in great demand, initially at St. Charles College in Grand Coteau, La (1886-87) and then in Galveston, Texas (1887-88). He was posted to Spring Hill College in Mobile, Ala as lamplighter, sacristan, handyman and back to his signature job, cook (1888-1900). He transferred his cooking assignment to the residence at Holy Name Rectory in New Orleans, adding to this job that of receptionist and manager of the common closet (1900-02). He returned to Spring Hill College for two years as the supervisor of the heating system, before resuming his favorite job, namely, cook (1902-09). After two years in Augusta, Ga, he began a long stint where he labored mainly as infirmarian (1911-24). In 1924 he arrived at the Novitiate in Grand Coteau to serve as infirmarian until 1934 when he returned to Spring Hill College, now as baker, assistant carpenter and maintenance man. He was in residence there from 1934 until 1947. Br. Richard J. Black, SJ died on August 31, 1947 in Mobile, a man of 80 years and 63 as a Jesuit Brother.

Br. Vincent Blatter, SJ
1836 – 1903

Vincent was born in Valais, Switzerland on July 19, 1836. He joined the New Orleans Mission on February 2, 1862. His first posting as a Brother was to Spring Hill College in Mobile, Ala where he showed aptitude for cooking, which he did for seven years (1870-74, 80-83) and then tended the college's horses and animals (1876-80). From there he went to the Jesuit residence in Augusta, Ga as sacristan, cook, dispenser of common items and receptionist (1883-85). He returned to Mobile to serve in the residence there as sacristan, cook, dispenser, receptionist and jack-of-all-trades (1886-89). He was sent back to Spring Hill College for eleven years where his labors are described as *ad domum*, that is, he served as the maintenance person assigned by Fr. Minister; and for five years he was also put in charge of the mules and horses of the college. In 1901 he was posted to St. Charles College in Grand Coteau, La where he was given the task of maintaining the barn of the college (1901-1903). In January of 1903, Br. Vincent Blatter, SJ died, 66 years old and 41 years a Jesuit Brother.

Br. Aloysius Boeni, SJ
1848 – 1929

Aloysius Boeni was born on February 18, 1848 in Ampten, Switzerland. Passing over gaps in his history, we know that he entered the Society on September 9, 1872. His records indicate that he spent two years as a scholastic novice, the path to priesthood. But in 1880 he traveled to Florissant, Mo to do his Novitiate as a Brother novice. He was sent to the college in New Orleans where he served as refectorian for three years (1880-83). His labors were concentrated on dining rooms and chapels. He moved to Grand Coteau, La to be sacristan and lamplighter from 1883 to 1895. He was then sent to the college in Galveston, Texas where he added several other tasks to what he had done in New Orleans, namely, infirmarian, house buyer, administrator of the clothing closet, and receptionist, tasks he performed from 1895 until 1913. He spent the next six years at Jesuit High School in Shreveport, La, performing the same tasks he had been doing all his life, with the addition of librarian (1913-19). Finally he moved to the college in Grand Coteau with his duties much reduced because of his age (1920-29). He was famous for holding four jobs at a time, despite the many maladies he suffered. Br. Aloysius Boeni, SJ died at Grand Coteau on December 9, 1929; he was 81 years old and 67as a Jesuit Brother. "A diary of Aloysius Boeni was discovered which confirms his spiritual resemblance to his sainted namesake" (Kenny, 192).

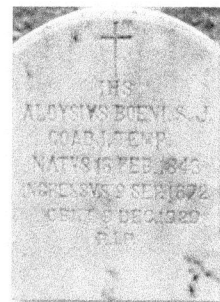

Br. Francis Bougnon, SJ
1870 – 1929

Francis was born in Montbéliard, France on March 15, 1870. After immigration to America, he entered the Society in Macon, Ga on August 7, 1890. Upon his vows, he was sent to Spring Hill College in Mobile, Ala for four years as its baker (1893-96). He returned to the Novitiate in Macon as its baker and also as the caretaker of its horses and mules (1897-99). He began a tour of the central establishments of the province, first Augusta, Ga (1899-1901), then Selma, Ala (1901-02), then Tampa , Fla (1902-04), then Spring Hill (1904-06). All the while he was baker and livestock caretaker, with carpentry and cooking added on. But with his assignment to Augusta, he undertook the maintenance of heating (1906-10). Back at Spring Hill for two years, he settled into the jobs of carpenter and furnace engineer. He spent four years at the high school in New Orleans doing the same tasks, but now with iron working added on (1912-16), the very jobs he continued to perform when he returned to Spring Hill College for two years. Recall that he was born in France, so it is not strange that he was sent to serve in Jesuit facilities in French Canada, although we have no record of what Francis did there (1918-21). He was sent to Grand Coteau for two years as its carpenter and iron-worker (1922-24). He returned to the Jesuit residence in Mobile doing a full slate of jobs, but no longer as carpenter and iron-worker (1924-27). He served one year at the Jesuit residence in Hot Springs, NC as porter, sacristan and refectorian. He finally retired, living a year at the Immaculate Conception in New Orleans (1928-29). Apparently Francis Bougnon, SJ moved then to Mobile where he died on May 27, 1929 at the age of 59 and 39 as a Jesuit Brother.

Br. Joseph Armand Brinkhaus, SJ
1859 – 1944

Joseph Armand Brinkhaus was born in Grand Coteau, La on June 22, 1859, within sight of St. Charles College where he was to spend most of his life. He was an honor student in the college there, until he entered the Novitiate shortly after his sixteenth birthday to begin his training as a Jesuit Brother.

One of his first assignments in this capacity was to help the field hands at the college's huge farm. It turned out, however, that their rough language and manner were not exactly conducive to a young novice's spiritual growth, and he was sent instead to work with Br. Cornelius Otten on various jobs. "Brother Joe," as he was affectionately called, was only nineteen when he assisted Brother Otten in the challenging work of building the parish church in Grand Coteau. They completed the structure in one year's time. Six years later, in 1886, Brother Joe was assigned the task of building the bell tower at the back of the church. It stands today as one of the most interesting structures in church architecture in that part of the country.

Although Joe Brinkhaus has been most widely know for his work in construction, he spent his sixty-nine years at the college in numerous other capacities. According to one record, he was a jack-of-all-trades and master of them all. Whatever he did, he did well. When given charge of the sugar mill, he turned out the best sugar the college had ever produced. As manager of the college farm for over sixty years, he corresponded regularly with Louisiana State University and the U.S. Department of Agriculture in Washington to acquaint himself with the most scientific, up-to-date methods of farming. So proficient was he, in fact, that many local old-timers who had farmed many more years than he, came to Grand Coteau to seek his advice and learn what he had been bold enough to try. Long before Gulf States Utilities supplied the countryside with electricity, Brother Joe installed a carbide gas system and later an electric dynamo and storage batteries to provide much-needed illumination. He was also an innovator in the areas of plumbing, corn-crushing, corn-milling, wood-sawing and pumping water.

Brother Joe was away from Grand Coteau for only one year of his life. In 1891, he and three other brothers went to New Orleans where they constructed a beautiful wooden church on St. Charles Avenue – the original Holy Name of Jesus Church, fifteen years before Loyola University was founded. Characteristic of everything he had done previously, the church was a solid and masterful piece of work. Thirty-one years later, it survived a trip across the Mississippi River to Westwego where it was reassembled and remained in use for approximately thirty more years.

In August of 1939, Brother Brinkhaus turned over the management of the farm to Brother Martial Lapeyre. He continued in his last years to help in whatever way he could. On March 7, 1944, Joseph Armand Brinkhaus SJ died peacefully in his room at St. Charles College, in the quiet little town where he had been born. Attending him at the time was his nephew, Dr. Armand Brinkhaus. The totality of his contributions was vast and the quality of his work always of the highest. He may not have traveled far from the place of his birth, but he mastered the art of blooming where he was planted. At his death he was 84 years old and a Jesuit Brother for 68 years.

Br. James Broderick, SJ
1872 – 1945

James Broderick was born in England on September 8, 1872, and entered the Order in Macon, Ga on September 7, 1892. His labors as a brother were all part of the well running of the houses to which he was stationed. Immediately after his vows, he was stationed at St. Charles College in Grand Coteau, La (1895-1901), where his principal tasks were receptionist, sacristan and buyer. In his last year at Grand Coteau he trained as an infirmarian. Then he was posted back to the Novitiate in Macon for four years (1901-05). While there, he also assigned the Novices their daily tasks. He was then sent to the college in New Orleans for six years (1905-11), at which time he became the refectorian for the institution. He was sent to Augusta, Ga to do all of the jobs he had been doing: receptionist, infirmarian, refectorian and visitor at prayer time am and pm (1911-16). Since schools seemed the best places for him, he moved to Galveston, Texas for two years, continuing the works he did in Augusta. Then he was sent back to the college in Grand Coteau (1918-22) to be infirmarian, then to New Orleans, both the school downtown and the university uptown, as infirmarian and refectorian. He had not seen Tampa, Fla yet, so he was posted there with lighter duties (1926-29), namely porter and sacristan. In 1929 he was missioned to Spring Hill College in Mobile, Ala in his typical capacity as infirmarian, porter, and keeper of the clothing closet. On July 26, 1945 Brother James Broderick, SJ died in New Orleans, 72 years old and 53 as a Jesuit Brother.

Br. Augustus Burchardt, SJ
1874 – 1909

Augustus Burchardt was born in Saxon, Germany on July 31, 1874 and entered the Order in Macon, Ga on September 15, 1892. His first assignment took him to the Jesuit church and mission in Selma, Ala where he served as cook and sacristan (1895-98). When he moved to Spring Hill College in Mobile, Ala, he served as the baker for the college for three years, as maintenance man, and engineer in charge of the heating system (1898-1902). After a cameo appearance in New Orleans, he was sent to Galveston, Texas as the house's handyman and lamplighter (1903-07). He returned to Georgia, first to Augusta as sacristan, infirmarian and the brother in charge of the clothing closet (1907-08) and then to Macon as carpenter (1908-09). It was in Macon that Augustus Burchardt died on January 23, 1909, at the youthful age of 36 and 17 as a Jesuit Brother.

Seated: Brs. Keller, Boemi, Steiner, ???
Standing: Brs. Burchardt, ??? , Henderson, Kiernan, Rittmeyer, Blenke, Brinkhaus

Br. Robert Burchardt, SJ
1872 – 1938

Robert was born in Breitenbach, Germany on October 20, 1872. His records tell us nothing about why and when he came to America. But the story picks up on September 13, 1891 when he entered the Novitiate in Macon, Ga. His first years as a Jesuit Brother demanded much of him as year-after-year for the first five years he had to learn a new skill: he began as the college's tailor and assistant baker; then he practiced carpentry, and then became the custodian of the heating system (1898-1904). He had now found his groove: he remained at Macon for twenty-two years, primarily as its tailor and custodian of the heating system (1898-1920). He was then posted to Spring Hill College in Mobile, Ala for nine years as the supervisor of the kitchen and general house manager (1921-29). He traveled to the high school in Shreveport, La, where for nine years, he was refectorian, supervisor of the kitchen, gardener, and assistant porter. In poor health Robert Burchardt, SJ was sent to the infirmary in Grand Coteau, La where he died on August 5, 1938, at the age of 65 and 42 as a Jesuit Brother.

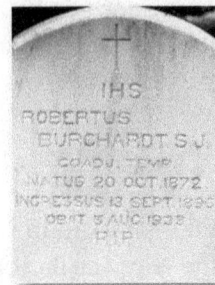

Br. Francis Buthod, SJ
1838 – 1910

From Savoy, Piedmont, came another Jesuit brother, Francis Buthod, who was born on November 24, 1838. He was nearly forty years old when he entered the Society of Jesus on September 6, 1877. He spent his first six years at St. Charles College in Grand Coteau, La as refectorian, assistant cook, and assistant librarian (1880-86). The next two years he served at the college in Galveston, Texas as associate cook, gardener, infirmarian and the person who distributed toiletries and clothing to the community (1886-88). After one year at Selma, Ala, Francis returned to Galveston for twenty-one years, namely, the rest of his life (1889-1910). His tasks were those he had done in his previous visit to Galveston. On November 10, 1910, Br. Francis Buthod, SJ died at the age of 72, having been a Jesuit Brother for 33 years.

Br. Hilary Castresana, SJ
1860 – 1940

Hilary Castresana was born at Mijala in Spain on October 21, 1860. Twenty-six years later, he emigrated to America and entered the Order at the Novitiate in Macon, Ga on November 12, 1886. He became a cook and served in that capacity for ten years, three years in Galveston, Texas (1888-1891) and seven years at the college in Grand Coteau, La (1891- 1898). But at this point in his service at Grand Coteau, he exchanged the role of cook for tailor and guardian of the clothing supply (1898-1902). He was moved to Spring Hill College in Mobile, Ala where he spent the next twenty years (1903-23), but with reduced duties, such as assistant baker, receptionist, and sacristan. In 1923 he was posted to Loyola University in New Orleans with the same duties

he had performed at Spring Hill (1923-1930). At this point he assumed a shepherd's role, namely disciplinarian for the young boys of the college and later he became the supervisor of the novice brothers and postulants in Grand Coteau (1930-1934). After this he served as refectorian and supervisor of the clothing room. After a year's posting to the high school in New Orleans, he returned to Grand Coteau for three years as the supervisor of the clothing room (1937-1940). Br. Hilary Castresana, SJ died on July 25, 1940; he was 80 years old and a Jesuit Brother for 54 years.

Br. William Cohnen, SJ
1859 – 1940

William Cohnen is another of the many Germans who emigrated to the United States in the last half of the nineteenth century and became Jesuit Brothers. He was born in Aachen, Germany on November 25, 1859. He subsequently entered the Jesuit Order at Florissant, Mo on October 24, 1884. After taking his vows he was sent to the college at Grand Coteau, La for eight years as its gardener to raise produce and vegetables for the students of the college (1886-94). He moved to the college in Galveston, Texas where he remained the vegetable gardener, with other tasks added to his schedule, such as lamplighter, sacristan, and the person in charge of the horses and mules of the institution (1894-1903). Then he headed east to Spring Hill College in Mobile, Ala to spend twenty-three years back in his first job of raising vegetables and produce for the college (1903-26). All the while he was also in charge of the maintenance for the Jesuit community. His last three years at Spring Hill College indicate that he was ageing and losing strength, for his only work is listed as the assistant clothing provider and assistant refectorian. In 1927 he retired to Grand Coteau, where for four years he continued being the community's handy-man. In Grand Coteau, in 1930, he is listed as infirm, a condition which existed for ten more years (1930-40). Br. William Cohnen, SJ died in New Orleans on April 17, 1940 at the age of 81 and 56 as a Jesuit Brother.

Br. Rombout DeVolder, SJ
1856 – 1899

Rombout DeVolder was born in Westrozeheim, Belgium on August 10, 1856, of a good Flemish family that named him for the Irish martyr who was the patron of St. Rombout's Cathedral, Malines. Rombout had training in woodcarving, watchmaking, and photography, when, tiring of these, he came to the United States to exploit his mechanical inventions. Finding that a trusted friend had patented some of these in his own name with much resulting profit, Rombuald concluded that this was God's way of telling him that the call he had resisted from early youth was the Lord's own voice. He was twenty-nine when he went to the Jesuits to ask admission as a coadjutor Brother, saying his hands were better than his head. Father Butler, who liked originals, had him enter the Florissant Novitiate in Missouri on November 12, 1885. He was transferred to the New Orleans Novitiate in Macon, Ga for his last year as a novice, where he remained one year as a cabinetmaker. Somewhere along the way, his Christian name was translated from Flemish, "Rombout," into French, "Rombould," and he was know thereafter by this name. At Macon he found happiness and spread it, doing the roughest and finest work with equal cheer, and his only trouble was on Sundays when his idle hands were itching for work but the Rector would not permit him even to mend shoes. So he toiled cheerily in various houses, his fine baritone often hymning with his carving for the Lord. Then, assigned to the same task, he served at Spring Hill College in Mobile, Ala from 1889 until 1891. He returned to New Orleans to work as part of the team of brothers who built the original Holy Name Church (1891-92). After its completion, Rombuald was sent to Grand Coteau, La for five years as its cabinetmaker (1892-97). He was posted to Jesuit High School in New Orleans as carpenter, which was to be his last assignment. Br. Rombuald DeVolder died on February 11, 1899, a young 43 years old and 14 as a Jesuit Brother.

Br. John Dougherty, SJ
1867 – 1935

John Dougherty was born in Glasgow, Scotland on June 1 1867. He went West, as many Europeans were doing, and eventually entered the Novitiate in Florissant, Mo on June 13, 1884. He is listed as having only one year of Novitiate, which must be an error, since the Society's law requires two and a half years. John seemed destined to carry a wooden spoon in his hand, because for eight years he was cook to some community or other as its refectorian. Although his first job was that of assistant cook at Jesuit High in New Orleans (1885-1886), he served as refectorian there for the next five years (1886-1892). He was assigned to the rectory at Holy Name in New Orleans where he resumed his job as cook for eight years, along with being the keeper of the common closet and the receptionist for the rectory (1892-1900). His services moved eastward in the province, three years in Augusta, Ga as porter and sacristan and seven at Spring Hill in Alabama. He went west again, this time to Jesuit High in New Orleans where he spent the last twenty years of his life. While his tasks were many, they were not burdensome. He became the assistant treasurer for the community, the man in charge of the clothes for the community, infirmarian and receptionist. At this time he was the assistant editor for "Church Calendar" (1925-1930). Obviously John had considerable schooling to be both treasurer and assistant editor. On June 12, 1935, John Dougherty, SJ died at the age of 68 and 51 as a Jesuit Brother.

Br. Benjamin Escher, SJ
1876 – 1938

Benjamin Escher was born on May 5, 1876 in Brig, Switzerland. He joined the Order in January 1896, but the earliest reference we have for him is in the catalogue of the Independent New Orleans Mission for 1898. He is listed at the Novitiate in Macon, Ga as the Brother in care of the barn, a job he did for four years; but the catalogue also lists his signature skill, namely the custodian of the college furnace (1889-1902). He was next posted to the Jesuit college in New Orleans as the boiler Brother, a task he performed for nine years (1904-12). When he was posted to Spring Hill College in Mobile, Ala, his exceptional abilities were employed not just as supervisor of the heating system, but as craftsman

in wood and iron and custodian of the wine cellar (1913-16). He was assigned to Jesuit High School in New Orleans, continuing his labors as the man in charge of the heating system, craftsman in wood and iron, and on a more domestic level, manager of the kitchen, to which was added the task of buyer (1916-28). It is briefly noted that he helped to produce the "Church Calendar." He then spent four years back at Spring Hill College, not only in charge of its heating system, but as its electrician (1928-32). His last posting was to Loyola University in New Orleans where because of his health, he was reduced in duties to that of sacristan (1932-38). On April 27, 1938, Br. Benjamin Escher, SJ died, 62 years old and 42 as a Jesuit Brother.

Br. Peter Fernandez, SJ
1864 – 1937

Peter Fernandez was born on June 29, 1864 in Guadalupe, Spain. After he immigrated to the United States, he entered the Novitiate in Macon, Ga on June 17, 1887. Soon after his Novitiate, he was sent to the college in Galveston, Texas, where his duties were that of cultivator of produce and vegetables for the college, infirmarian, lamplighter and sacristan (1890-94). From there he was sent to the college in Grand Coteau, La where his primary job was that of refectorian (1894-1900). When he was transferred to the college in New Orleans he continued to serve as the refectorian (1900-05). Peter returned to Galveston for two years, now as the cook (1905-07). Continuing his tour of the province, he traveled to the school in Shreveport, La where his jobs were that of cook, refectorian, and curator of the common closet (1907-11). Then he was off to Tampa, Fla for two years in the same capacity in which he generally served (1911-13). After one year in New Orleans, Peter returned to Shreveport, where he continued to be cook, refectorian and keeper of the common closet, to which was added that of infirmarian (1913-20). This peripatetic brother went back to Galveston for a year, then to Macon for another year and finally back to Tampa where he served as cook, sacristan and doorkeeper (1922-29). The records indicate that while he was posted to the high school in Tampa, he resided for four years in the Jesuit residence in Ybor City, the Cuban part of Tampa for which his Spanish was an apostolic plus. Finally he was sent to Grand Coteau where he served for three years in maintenance and then five years in the infirmary in poor health (1929-32, 1933-37). Br. Peter Fernandez, SJ died on April 29, 1937, 73 years old and 50 years a Jesuit.

Br. Edmund Freret, SJ
1846 – 1920

Edmund Freret was born in New Orleans on May 4, 1846. His career as a Jesuit began in St. Louis, Mo where he entered the Society as a scholastic novice in 1870. He went to Grand Coteau, La where he both taught the younger students at the college and began his own college study of letters (1872-76). As was the custom, he transferred to Spring Hill College in Mobile, Ala for two years of philosophy (1876-78). At this point in his Jesuit life he switched vocation tracks from that of a scholastic novice to that of a Brother novice (1878). Inasmuch as the New Orleans Mission was then under the jurisdiction of the Lyons province, Edmund was sent to their schools in the Middle East where he spent the next twenty-four years of his life. Many Catholics in the Middle East spoke French, as did Edmund.

His first posting was to the College of St. Joseph in Beirut, Syria where he taught English and was the associate librarian (1878-82). He was assigned for fifteen years to the Francis Xavier College being built in Alexandria, Egypt; he taught little there as his tasks became those associated with the food service of the college: refectorian, keeper of the cellar and of the common closet (1882-97). After a year in Constantine, Algeria (1897-99), he spent two years at at Saint-Étienne in France (1899-1901). He then went to England to serve at St. Mary's College in Canterbury, Kent (1902-07), and then to Hastings (1907-12).With passport ever current, Edmund spent two years at the College of St. Francis in Bollengo, Italy (1912-15), then returned to France for four years at the college in Lyons (1915-19). He had hardly returned to Italy when Br. Edmund Freret, SJ died in Bollengo, Italy on August 15, 1920, at 74 years of age and 50 years as a Jesuit Brother.

Br. Joseph Garbely, SJ
1822 – 1895

Joseph Garbely was born in Valais, Switzerland on February 5, 1822. He traveled to America as part of the New Orleans Mission of the Lyons Province, and entered the Society in Macon, Ga on September 8, 1861. He apparently came from a farming background, for he was put in charge of the horses and mules at St. Charles College in Grand Coteau, La (1862-69). He was also in charge of the college's barns and he practiced carpentry in addition. For the rest of his Jesuit life he was assigned to Spring Hill College in Mobile, Ala (1870-93),where he continued to care for the college's animals and its barns. To this were added domestic tasks, such as charge of the wine cellar; he dispensed the common items to the community; and he regularly served as carpenter. His last years found him reassigned to the care of the animals. Br. Joseph Garbely, SJ died on May 16, 1895, 73 years old and 34 years a Jesuit Brother.

Br. Paschal Gil, SJ
1869 – 1944

Paschal Gil was born in Murcia, Spain on January 2, 1869. Long before he was twenty years old, he entered the Novitiate in Macon, Ga on June 17, 1887. But as a Jesuit Brother he spent the next 54 years of his life at Spring Hill College in Mobile, Ala (1890-1944). Except for Br. Joseph Brinkhaus, Pascal Gil served the longest of any Jesuit in the same place. At first he served as refectorian, but then became sacristan of the institution, and for one year he was the baker for the college (1896-97). His most consistent job was that of keeper of the clothing closet, which he did for thirty years (1898-1928). By 1929, Paschal had his duties reduced to sacristan, which he continued for thirteen years (1929-42). He moved from Jesuit residence of the college to the separate Jesuit residence where he lived for two more years. On June 24, 1944, Br. Paschal Gil, SJ died at 75 years of age and 57 as a Jesuit Brother.

Br. Antonio Gros, SJ
1847 – 1917

Antonio, a native of Barcelona, Spain, was born on December 12, 1847. He entered the Aragon Province on August 14, 1874. Shortly after, he embarked for the New Mexico/ Colorado Mission, where he labored for the rest of his life. Little is recorded of his life except that he took his final vows on August 15, 1884. Like most Brothers on the frontier, he was adept at many jobs. His death notice in the Naples Province records describes him as pious and a lover of labor. On November 22, 1917 Br. Antonio Gros, SJ died: he was seventy-eight years old and forty- three a Jesuit brother. He is buried in El Paso, Texas in the Jesuit section of Concordia Cemetery.

Br. John Gros, SJ
1848 – 1910

In Savoy, Piedmont, John Gros was born on April 15, 1848. He was in his mid thirties when he entered the Order in Florissant, Mo on October 30, 1882. His first assignment was that of refectorian at the college in New Orleans (1884-86). He was then sent to the college at Grand Coteau, La first as refectorian for one year, but as its cook for thirteen years (1887-1900). Equipped with knives and spoons, he brought his cooking skills to the Jesuit residence in Augusta, Ga, where he served as cook and refectorian (1900-06). When moved to Shreveport, La, he continued as cook, refectorian, and keeper of the clothing closet. Then he was posted to the college in Galveston, Texas, where for three years he continued to serve as cook. On February 14, 1910, Br. John Gros, SJ died in Galveston, sixty-three years of age and twenty-eight as a Jesuit Brother.

Br. Salvator Hellin, SJ
1869 – 1931

Salvator Hellin was born on August 13, 1869 in Murcia, Spain. As a young man he entered the Novitiate at Macon, Ga on September 16, 1888. He was apparently a competent refectorian, for he served in that job at the college in New Orleans from 1891 to 1900. When transferred to Spring Hill College in Mobile, Ala, he became a baker for the school for six years (1900-06). He was sent to the Jesuit residence in Tampa, Fla, moving his cooking skills from the oven to the top of the stove (1908-11). He served in Shreveport, La for three years as cook, keeper of the clothing closet and the common room. (1911-14). He moved to the newly established Loyola University in New Orleans to be cook, refectorian and general factotum (1914-17). He returned to the high school in Tampa for four years as supervisor of the kitchen and as refectorian (1917-21). He went back into the kitchen as cook in Galveston, Texas where he also cultivated produce for the table (1921-24). Finally he was given a shot at the Jesuit institutions in New Orleans. Although in residence at Jesuit High School, he was made cook for Manresa Retreat House located at that time in New Orleans, eventually residing there (1926-31). As the number of retreats kept rising, so too the number of men he served. Br. Salvator Hellin, SJ died in New Orleans on May 10, 1931. He was seventy-two years old and a Jesuit Brother for forty-three years.

Br. Aloysius Imsand, SJ
1865 – 1935

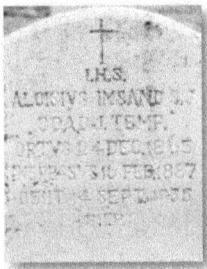

On Christmas Eve 1865, another future Jesuit Brother was born in Ulrichen, Switzerland, namely Aloysius Imsand. He was twenty-two years old when he entered the New Orleans Mission in Macon, Ga on February 16, 1887. His first assignment was to the farm at Grand Coteau, La where he was in charge of the barn for six years (1889-95). Cattle and dairy were ably attended by Aloysius. He moved to Spring Hill College in Mobile, Ala to serve as the caretaker of the college's animals for ten years (1895-1905), which suggests that when Aloysius was growing up back in Ulrichen, he was probably a farmer who ran a dairy and tended animals. He returned to the college at Grand Coteau where he once more tended its cattle and dairy animals for twenty-nine years (1905-35). He is often listed as also working in the garden to grow produce for the college and foods for his animals. And occasionally he was the custodian of the wine cellar. Br. Aloysius Imsand, SJ died in New Orleans on September 14, 1935 at the age of seventy years and a Jesuit Brother for forty-eight years.

Brothers at St. Charles College, Grand Coteau, La – ca. 1895
Standing: Brs. Hannon, Imsand, Sauzéat, Locher
Seated: Brs. Brinkhaus, Steiner, King, Sengghen, Boemi

Br. Francis Imsand, SJ
1834 – 1909

Francis was born on October 20, 1834 in Valais, Switzerland. At the age of twenty-six, he joined the New Orleans Mission on February 2, 1861. After his Novitiate he remained at St. Charles College in Grand Coteau, La for many more years, indeed his entire life as a Jesuit Brother (1861-1909). His signature job was that of infirmarian of the college and community. Occasionally he was asked to include other tasks, such as dispenser of common items (thirteen years), keeper of the wine cellar (four years), and caretaker of the college's poultry (once). Our records unfortunately tell us nothing about the character of this man, his piety and industry. What we do know is that he died on March 17, 1909, seventy-four years old and forty-eight a Jesuit Brother.

Br. Francis Jost, SJ
1842 – 1921

Francis was another Swiss, born in Obergesteln on September 26, 1842. He entered the Novitiate in Macon, Ga on February 2, 1861 just shy of his nineteenth birthday. He was first posted to Spring Hill College in Mobile, Ala. And from 1871 to 1884 he was the sacristan at the college in New Orleans. When transferred back to Spring Hill College, he was assigned a wide variety of tasks: lamplighter, infirmarian, keeper of the clothes closet, house manager, assistant treasurer and buyer for the house; he was in charge of the wine cellar for eleven years. In all, except for the few years at Grand Coteau, he served at Spring Hill for thirty-six years. The range of his abilities clearly suggests that he was a literate person. Br. Francis Jost, SJ died at Spring Hill College on June 10, 1921 at the age of seventy-nine years old and sixty years a Jesuit Brother.

Br. Stephen Keller, SJ
1859 – 1941

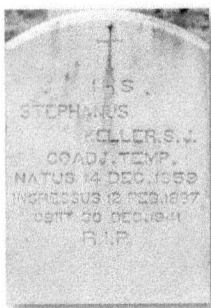

Stephen Keller, who was born on December 14, 1859 in Marienweiler;, Germany, was another of the many German emigrants to come to America and join the Society of Jesus. He entered the Novitiate in Macon, Ga on February 12, 1887, when he was twenty-eight years old. After his formation, he remained at the Macon Novitiate for six years; he either was already or he learned quickly to be a tailor, as well as the keeper of the common closet. He took his sartorial skills to Spring Hill College in Mobile, Ala from 1895 until 1901. At this point Stephen returned to Macon to spend twenty-one years doing the same tasks he had done previously, with the addition of also being the receptionist (1901-22). For a change, Stephen was posted to Grand Coteau, La to continue for twenty more years in his signature talent, namely, tailor (1922-41). Br. Stephen Keller, SJ died in a hospital in Lafayette on December 30, 1941. He was eighty-two years old and a Jesuit Brother for fifty-four.

Br. Joseph A. Leunda, SJ
1851 – 1908

Joseph Leunda was born on December 2, 1851. At the age of thirty-four, he entered the Order on October 29, 1886. It appears that from 1900 on, he spent the rest of his life as a Jesuit Brother at the residence of Sacred Heart Church in Tampa. Fla, doing the following tasks: sacristan, dispenser of common items, buyer for the house and caretaker of the clothing of its residents. On February 22, 1908, Br. Joseph A. Leunda, SJ died at the age of fifty-seven and twenty-two years a Jesuit.

Br. Damaso Lezama, SJ
1867 – 1922

Although Damaso Lezama was born in San Salvador, Spain on December 10, 1867, he was fated to become a Jesuit in North America. When he was almost twenty years old, he entered the Novitiate in Macon, Ga on July 14, 1886. The premier service Damaso rendered was that of cook. For four years he was the chef of the community in Grand Coteau, La (1889-93). For nine years he labored at the college in Galveston, Texas as cook (1893-1902); along with being the cook at Shreveport, La, he was dispenser of the common toiletries, buyer for the community and keeper of the common closet (1902-06). He was posted for three years to the Jesuit residence in Augusta, Ga where besides serving as its cook, he was also refectorian (1906-09). Damaso was finally sent to the college in Grand Coteau where he spent the last thirteen years of his life, no longer as cook, but now with less taxing tasks. In 1921, he retired to the infirmary where he spent his final weeks. On January 14, 1922, Br. Damaso Lezama, SJ died, at the age of fifty-five and thirty-six as a Jesuit Brother.

Br. Wendelin Locher, SJ
1850 – 1926

In the small village of Bratsch, Switzerland, Wendelin Locher was born on April 17, 1850. He entered the Novitiate at Florissant, Mo on December 2, 1882. His first assignment was to the college in Grand Coteau, La to train and serve as its baker (1884-89). He then went to Spring Hill College, Mobile, Ala to tend to another metal hot-box, not an oven but the college's heating system, a task he performed for twelve years (1889-1901). He was the maintenance man for the college all these years. He was then posted for four years to the Jesuit residence in Augusta, Ga where he continued his care-taking of the heating system (1902-06), and then it was back to Spring Hill College from 1906 until 1909, first as manager of the heating system but also was a worker in iron (blacksmith?). Wendelin returned to Augusta where he labored for eleven years, not only caring for the heating system, but also as refectorian, keeper of the clothing closet, sacristan, dispenser of the common supplies, gardener and manager of the kitchen (1915-26). His tasks seemed heavy in the eyes of others, who considered them too strenuous and inappropriate to an aging man. But nobody consulted him. Br. Wendelin Locher, SJ died at Spring Hill College on October 18, 1926; he was seventy-six years old and forty-four years a Jesuit Brother.

Br. Innocent Meaza, SJ
1866 – 1920

On December 28, 1866, Innocent Meaza was born in Orozko, Spain. Just shy of his twentieth birthday, he entered the Novitiate at Macon, Ga on December 19, 1885. After taking his vows, he was assigned to the college in New Orleans as apprentice cook and then head cook. This was his primary assignment for most of his Jesuit life, namely twenty-six years as king of the kitchen. He also dispensed the common supplies of the community. Eventually he served in another institution of

the province, the college at Grand Coteau, La, but no longer as cook (1914-20). His lighter duties were those which pertained to the chapels, domestic and collegiate. Br. Innocent Meaza, SJ died on March 7, 1920, fifty-three years old and thirty-five years as a Jesuit Brother.

Br. Frederick Melder, SJ
1860 – 1929

Frederick Melder was born in Freiburg, Baden-Württemberg on August 14, 1860. He entered the Macon, Ga Novitiate on February 12, 1887. He seemed destined to serve in the kitchens of various communities in the province, because Frederick became the baker for the college in Grand Coteau, La from 1888 until 1892. He was transferred to Spring Hill College in Mobile, Ala as its assistant cook (1892-99). Then he served the Tampa, Fla community as its cook for three years (1899-1902). He was posted to the Jesuit community in Selma, Ala for three years as its cook (1902-05). Still in Alabama, he headed south to Spring Hill College to spend the last twenty-four years of his life. The closest he got to the kitchen there was his job as refectorian. Indirectly he was attached to the kitchen because of his labors as an assistant gardener growing food for the college. His last eight years at Spring Hill were spent in a state of declining health (1921-29). When Br. Frederick Melder, SJ died on September 11, 1929 he was sixty-nine years old and forty-two a Jesuit Brother.

Br. Raymond Mendizabal, SJ
1880 – 1921

Raymond Mendizabal was born on January 11, 1880 in San Sebastian, Spain. The New Orleans Mission was quickly morphing into the New Orleans Province when he entered the Order at Macon, Ga on August 14, 1900. After pronouncing his vows, he remained at the house of probation in Macon for eighteen years, namely, the rest of his Jesuit life. For sixteen of those years he served as the beadle of the postulants and novices. Yet his contribution was also made to the community as infirmarian for fourteen years and as manager of the storeroom where small things for personal use were kept. All the while he was available as the community's maintenance man as need arose. He was a mere forty-one years old when he died on September 29, 1921; he was twenty-one years a Jesuit Brother.

Br. James Mengus, SJ
1822 – 1899

James Mengus was born in Rosenwiller, France on July 25, 1822. He traveled to the United States to join the New Orleans Mission and entered the Novitiate on April 9, 1859. After his training at Grand Coteau, La, he remained there for four years in maintenance work. He was transferred to Spring Hill College in Mobile, Ala, where he labored from 1866 to 1878. He was sometimes the baker for the college, but his regular work was in the fields cultivated by the college for its food. He returned to the college at Grand Coteau in continuation of his success as farmer who grew the college's food. (1879-1884). He returned to Spring Hill College in the same capacity he formerly had, namely, the brother in charge of food production (1884-1897). But by his mid-seventies he was no longer able to labor in the fields and was classified as a Jesuit who had retired because of his health. Br. James Mengus, SJ died on November 8, 1899, seventy-eight years old and forty-one as a Jesuit Brother.

Br. Peter Morge, SJ
1846 – 1902

In Gelles, France, Peter Morge was born on March 12, 1846. He entered the Society on November 19, 1866 at Macon, Ga. He served as cabinetmaker at the college in New Orleans (1883-89), and then became the general maintenance man, first at Spring Hill in Alabama (1889-1890) and then at the Macon Novitiate (1890-91). Br. Peter traveled to New Orleans to work as part of the team which built the original Holy Name Church (1891-92). In 1899 he arrived in Galveston, Texas, where his carpentry skills were required again (1899-1901). Finally he returned to New Orleans where he kept on carving for a New Orleans shrine until June 23, 1902, when he put his tools in his chest, cleaned up his room, and went to the Rector's office, and said: "Mon Père, c'est la mort" ("My Father, I am dying"). He had entered the Society in his native France in his twenty-first year, 1866, and French remained his spiritual medium. Father Maring (rector) understood and appreciated this fact. Br. Peter Morge, SJ, "blessed with all sacramental graces, departed within the hour to enjoy, we may assume, the artistries of heaven" (Kenny, 164). He was fifty-six years old and thirty-six years a Jesuit Brother.

Jesuits in New Orleans 1887
Left to right: Brs. Peter Morge, John Dougherty, Ignatius Boemecke, Ferdinand Peter,
Fr. Rector John O'Connor, Fr. Minister Argué, Brs. Joseph Montegazzi, Bernard Schwartz, Anthony Müller

Br. Anthony Müller, SJ
1845 – 1921

On January 21, 1845, Anthony Müller was born in Urspringen, Bavaria. He was in his early twenties when he entered the Novitiate in Macon, Ga on December 24,1867. His beginning years in the Society determined the kinds of service he was to render: alternating between Grand Coteau, La and Spring Hill College in Alabama from 1869 to 1879, he became skilled as tailor and as one who preserved and distributed clothing. He was later posted to the college at Grand Coteau to serve as sacristan, receptionist and tailor (1880-83). He spent his next six years at the college in New Orleans as tailor and keeper of the common closet (1883-89). Back in Grand Coteau, his primary duty for the next eighteen years was that of tailor, as well as buyer for the house, keeper of the common closet, and receptionist (1889- 1907). He had two years off from the college as he was sent for one year to the high school in Shreveport to perform his signature tasks, and one year to Augusta, doing many tasks, except that of tailor (1907-09). He then returned to Grand Coteau as its chief tailor, who also attended to the wine cellar and dispensed items from the common source (1909-21). His duties lightened with age, to the point that he was only a tailor. Br. Anthony Müller, SJ died on March 25, 1921 at the age of seventy-six and a Jesuit Brother for fifty-four years.

Br. Francis Nolte, SJ
1857 – 1903

"Fish River" Alabama, while not a particularly famous place, nevertheless was where Francis Nolte was born on August 17, 1857. It took thirty-two years for Francis to make his decision to join the New Orleans Mission and so to enter the Society in Macon, Ga on February 21, 1888. He remained at the Novitiate for four more years, serving as the gardener and one year as infirmarian (1888-94). He spent one year at the college in New Orleans as the infirmarian (1894-95). Francis then traveled west to Grand Coteau, La where he continued his gardening, as well as buying for the community and dispensing common items (1895-1900). He was posted to Spring Hill College in Mobile, Ala as gardener and custodian of the farm animals (1900-02), and returned to Macon now as its gardener and the manager of its barn. Br. Francis Nolte, SJ died on February 2, 1903 at forty-five years old and fifteen as a Jesuit Brother.

Br. Cornelius Otten, SJ
1835 – 1916

On March 12, 1835, Cornelius Otten was born in Ginneken, a town in North Brabant, a province of the Netherlands. He entered the Society on August 14, 1855 and continued to be trained in carpentry and cabinetmaking. Although Cornelius was renowned for his building skills, he is the only Brother listed in the province catalogue up to this time to teach catechism for seven years in the local church (1867-74). His fame in the province derives from his activities as a builder, which skill he mastered at the college in Grand Coteau, La (1867-84). His first major project was the parish church at

Grand Coteau. The plans were drawn up by the famous New Orleans architect, James Freret, in 1875. Brothers Otten and Brinkhaus began the construction in 1879 and the church was blessed in 1880.

In 1884 Otten was transferred from Grand Coteau to Galveston, Texas where the Society had received a parish and school (St. Mary's University) that same year. In this new foundation he did just about everything. He is listed as sacristan, buyer, carpenter and *ad omnia*. In the early years he supervised the renovation of one of the school buildings into a chapel. The Society engaged the services of Nicholas J. Clayton, still famous as one of Victorian Galveston's greatest architects, to design a new church. In 1889 Otten directed the construction of the French Romanesque structure.

> The expense was also much reduced by the builder, Brother Cornelius Otten, SJ, an architect of like mind, who was also a master of every trade and craft. Working harmoniously together, they built a great turreted, high-domed, grandly windowed temple, harmonized within and without to every artistic and liturgical demand. It was 155 feet in length, 65 in the aisles and 90 in the transept, and the Cross in its circling dome rose 125 feet above the Gulf (Kenny, 133).

In 1897 Otten was transferred to Augusta, Ga where he began to erect a new church more or less on the lines of Clayton's plans, but smaller. That same design was followed loosely in Macon, Ga and Tampa, Fla where Otten continued in 1899 and 1902 to construct new churches. After some years in Key West, Fla and Spring Hill, Alabama, Brother Otten was recalled to Grand Coteau in 1907 to supervise the rebuilding of the college which had burned down in 1900. The job was completed in 1909. But Brother Otten was then 74. He was an exceptional craftsman; he worked alongside the construction crews and arranged treats for them as an incentive for sound craftsmanship and Christian living. He impressed all with his piety and, though his skills were of a high professional order, he never shrank from the humblest tasks. Everyone had a good word to say about this edifying Brother. He made himself useful around Grand Coteau until his death on June 6, 1916, at the age of eighty-one and sixty-one as a Jesuit Brother.

Br. John Pfeiler, SJ
1871 – 1914

John Pfeiler was born in Neukirch, Germany on August 24, 1871. After emigrating and settling in America, he entered the Novitiate in on October 8, 1893. After his formation, he remained at Macon, Ga learning a craft that became his signature job for the rest of his life, namely, cooking. First he served as apprentice cook for two years and then chief chef for fourteen years there. Except for the job of waking up the community in the morning, he labored as its cook. Br. John Pfeiler, SJ died on November 29, 1914; he was just forty-three years old and a Jesuit Brother for twenty-one.

Br. Francis Quaranta, SJ
1876 – 1941

Francis Quaranta was born in Grottaglie, Italy on September 4, 1876. He entered the Order on September 28, 1904 in Macon. The first part of his life was spent in Albuquerque, New Mexico where he served at St. Felipe Neri Church. For three years, his job at St. Felipe was custodian/sacristan of the church and keeper of the common clothes closet. He moved to the residence of the Immaculate Conception in Albuquerque where he again attended to the order of the church and served as refectorian. When he was sent to Jesuit High School in New Orleans, he acquired new skills such as engineer of the heating system, carpenter and iron worker, at which he worked for nine years (1927-34). He served in Grand Coteau, La as janitor of the parish church and keeper of food stuffs. After one year at Manresa in Louisiana (1939-40), Br. Francis Quaranta, SJ returned to the province infirmary in Grand Coteau, where he died on April 22, 1941. He was seventy-five years old and thirty-seven a Jesuit Brother.

Br. Francis Rickard, SJ
1882 – 1951

Although many famous people have been born in Palestine, the New Orleans Province acknowledges Francis A. Rickard as born on October 4, 1882 in Palestine, Texas, that is. He entered the Novitiate in Macon, Ga in 1899, and stayed on there to become its kitchen czar for five years (1901-05). When posted to Spring Hill College in Mobile, Ala, he continued as culinary king for five more years (1906-12). Francis then spent six years at Grand Coteau, La reigning over the college's kitchen (1916-22). He went back to Spring Hill where he returned to his old position as czar of pots and pans for five years (1922-27). He spent only one year back at Macon in his signature job (1927-28), before beginning a stay of ten years at the high school in New Orleans in a job with which he was all too familiar. After six more years of KP, Francis was assigned as the brother socius to the provincial for four years and was made the prefect of the library (1928-38). He moved up town to Loyola University, now caring for the clothing closet instead of the ovens (1939-41). He was sent in 1941 to Jesuit High in Shreveport, La and in 1942 to Jesuit High New Orleans. In 1944, he returned to Grand Coteau, where his duties became easy and his burdens light; he became receptionist and sacristan and maker of the Eucharistic breads. On February 23, 1951, Br. Francis Rickard, SJ died at sixty-nine years of age and fifty years as a Jesuit Brother.

Br. Henry Rittmeyer, SJ
1864 – 1929

Henry was born in Nesselröden, Germany on March 5, 1864. He emigrated to the United States which was just recovering from its Civil War, and entered the Society at Florissant, Mo on July 31, 1880 at the salad age of sixteen. He headed South for his first assignment, a "brother for all tasks," to the college in New Orleans. When he entered the Order he manifested no particular skill or trade, so it was a while until the Society found the right jobs for him. When assigned to Spring Hill College in Mobile, Ala he found his kingdom in the kitchen. He became assistant cook for four years, as well as its baker for five years (1884-93). He was sent to the college in Grand Coteau, La where for seven years he served as the cook. Cooks need stuff to cook, and so for six years he added gardener to his job (1893-1907). After a one-year stay at Spring Hill as cook, he returned to the college at Grand Coteau for twenty years (1908-28). His new jobs kept him out of the kingdom of the kitchen, except for the few years when he was the brother in charge of the guests' dining room, refectorian or supervisor of the kitchen. But he remained the official gardener, growing produce for the meals of the students and faculty of the college.

Henry Rittmeyer belonged to the Jesuit dynasty of Boemeckes and Marings from Germany and was the blood brother of Father George Rittmeyer, who joined the faculty at St. Charles College in Grand Coteau in 1872. "They number fifteen good Jesuits of three generations in every service of our province, descendants of one loyal Catholic couple in the Protestant-circled village of Catholic Nessel-röden" (Kenny 159). Br. Henry Rittmeyer, SJ was assigned to Hot Springs, NC in 1928 where he died on New Year's Day 1929. Henry was only sixty-five years old, but forty-nine as a Jesuit Brother.

Br. Bernard Schwartz, SJ
1866 – 1936

In the small town of Wesel, Germany, Bernard Schwartz was born on November14, 1866. He was 18 years old when he entered the Novitiate in Florissant, Mo on March 10, 1884. It often takes a few years for a brother to learn a skill suitable to him and valuable to the Society. Bernard tried out several: sacristan for one year, infirmarian for four, and receptionist for three years; he was listed mostly as maintenance man for the residence (1885-88).When he was assigned to Macon, Ga, he trained as a tailor, a craft he practiced for eleven years, and was posted for eight years to Spring Hill (1892-1900). He became the assistant to the house treasurer and the brother in charge of dispensing toiletries, etc. When he moved West to the college at Grand Coteau, La, he began to serve primarily as infirmarian, although his tasks included those of refectorian, house buyer and receptionist (1901-18). He then spent three years at the college in Galveston, Texas, basically continuing his skill as infirmarian and refectorian (1918-21). He spent two years at the Jesuit residence in Augusta, Ga doing his two signature services, as well as custodian of the clothing closet (1922-24). He was posted then to Loyola University for seven years, then to Jesuit High School in the same city for two years, and finally to the residence of the Immaculate Conception Church in downtown New Orleans (1924-36). Of course he was infirmarian all this time, but there is a notice that he was the designated table reader at Loyola for a while. This confirms that, although German-born, he was literate enough to read English to a university faculty. He must have been a pleasant person, for he kept being assigned to act as receptionist. Br. Bernard Schwartz, SJ died on July 24, 1936, eighty years old and fifty two as a Jesuit brother.

Br. Louis Sempé, SJ
1867 – 1927

Louis Sempé was born in Tarbes, France on March 19, 1867. When he was twenty-years old, he entered the Novitiate at St. Joseph's House, Slough, England on March 12, 1887. He transferred to the House of Formation in Macon, Ga to complete his Novitiate. When sent to Spring Hill College in Mobile, Ala, he was for eighteen years the lamplighter of the school's buildings and, for five years the assistant prefect of the library (1890-1908); all this while he served in the school as its "utility" Brother who did various jobs as needed. For the next eighteen years, he served at Jesuit High New Orleans, returning to his job as assistant prefect of the library for two years and all the while refectorian of the school (1909-27). Br. Louis Sempé, SJ died on July 15, 1927 at the age of sixty and forty as a Jesuit Brother.

Br. Leo Sengghen, SJ
1841 – 1916

In Obergesteln, Switzerland, Leo Sengghen was born on July 18, 1841. He entered the Order on January 12, 1877. He must have entered the Society with a background in farming and animal husbandry, because from 1880 he is listed as plying this craft for the next nineteen years. He did this job for eight years at the college in Grand Coteau, La (1881-89) and for eight years at the house of formation in Macon, Ga (1890-98). In the same capacity he returned to Grand Coteau for two years (1898-1900). While at Grand Coteau, although his focus remained on animals and food production, his task was modified as he was put in charge of the college's horses and mules for four years. In 1905, the Society took him from the fields and placed him in the dining room, where he served as refectorian for the next eleven years (1905-16). Br. Leo Sengghen, SJ died on September 19, 1916 at the age of seventy-five and a Jesuit Brother for thirty-nine years.

Br. John Steiner, SJ
1853 – 1943

John Steiner was born in Erschmatt, Switzerland on October 12, 1853. He was part of the Swiss migration to the United States in the second half of the nineteenth century. When he was twenty years old, he entered the Society on March 1, 1873 at Grand Coteau, La. From 1873 until 1913 he exercised his skill as cook for various communities. For nine years at Grand Coteau, his primary and only job was cooking (1880-89), and when moved to the Jesuit residence in Mobile, Ala, he continued to cook for twenty-five more years (1889-1914). In this smaller institution, he was also assigned other duties, such as sacristan, dispenser of common articles, and receptionist. He was sent to the college at Grand Coteau, but no longer as a cook; his duties became much lighter, namely, sacristan, assistant receptionist and gardener (1914-22). When the college metamorphosed into a house of formation, he remained for six more years on light duty (1922-28). Finally, he was posted to Spring Hill College, where for the next fourteen years his sole task was that of the community's maintenance man (1929-43). Br. John Steiner, SJ died at the age of eighty-nine on September 26, 1943. He had been a Jesuit Brother for seventy full years.

Br. Joseph Todt, nSJ
1872 – 1893

All we know of this man is where he was born: Arnsberg, Germany. He entered the Novitiate at Macon, Ga but he died in the first year of his noviceship, August 29, 1893, at the age of twenty-one but not yet a full year in the Society.

Br. Oscar J. Wocet, SJ
1868 – 1931

Oscar Wocet might be the only person from Bohemia to enter the New Orleans Province. He was born in Neveklov, Bohemia on April 16, 1868, and entered the Novitiate in Macon, Ga on September 13, 1887 as a scholastic novice. Hence he followed the path of formation for Jesuit priesthood, including juniorate (1889), philosophy (1890-93), regency at St. Charles College in Grand Coteau, La (1893-97), and theology (1897-1900). At that point in his Jesuit life he decided to become a Jesuit Brother and went to the Novitiate in Florissant, Mo for his formation as a Brother. He was obviously well trained for academic work, and so he began to make the rounds of the schools of the province, specializing in the teaching of French. First, he taught French for three years at the Jesuit college in Galveston, Texas, where he also preached in the Church (1901–04). He returned to the site of his regency at the college in Grand Coteau for one year (1904-05). He was transferred to another of the province's colleges, Spring Hill in Mobile, Ala, where in addition to teaching French, he taught English (1905-19). Apparently he suffered some ailment which side-tracked him for a number of years. Finally he was called even higher, to Loyola University in New Orleans, where he spent the last twelve years of his life. No more classroom for Oscar; his duties were much reduced to assistant treasurer and prefect of the library (1919-31). Br. Oscar J. Wocet, SJ died on August 21, 1931; he was sixty-three years old and forty-four a Jesuit Brother.

Br. Francis Zuber, SJ
1854 – 1926

Francis Zuber was born on October 29, 1854 in the Swiss town of Brig. He was nineteen when he entered the Novitiate at Macon, Ga on March 1, 1873. Afterwards, he was posted to the college in Grand Coteau, La. In his early life as a brother, his specialty craft was baking, first at the college in Grand Coteau for four years, and then for three years at Spring Hill College in Mobile, Ala. Growing parallel to baking was his skill as an infirmarian which he practiced for fifteen years at Spring Hill (1884-99). He moved along with his competency as an infirmarian to the college in New Orleans where he spent the next twenty-seven years (1899-1926). To be sure, his heavier dues were lightened by the appearance of a younger infirmarian and his tasks were reduced to that of receptionist. Br. Francis Zuber, SJ died on December 3, 1926, at the age of seventy-two and a Jesuit Brother for fifty-three.

**Unidentified Brothers at
St. Charles College,
Grand Coteau, La
ca. 1903**

The Wave that Crested and Receded

Several things characterize this last phase of the history of the Jesuit Brothers. First, there is the remarkable rise and fall of the number of Jesuits in the New Orleans Province.

	Priests	Scholastics	Brothers	Total
1930	188	124	37	349
1950	289	206	38	533
1965	342	231	61	634
1980	362	73	41	476
2000	250	36	28	317
2014	184	44	14	242

Despite the Great Depression and World War II, the province had the resources and manpower to move into new apostolic works. Actually, the works taken up were not so much new in character as new in the number of parishes and schools in the care of the province: "more of the same."

Parishes up to 1930	*Colleges and Universities*	*High Schools*
6 parishes	Loyola University	Jesuit High New Orleans
	Spring Hill College	Spring Hill College High School
	Sacred Heart College	St. John Berchmans
	University of St. Mary	Jesuit High Tampa
	St. Charles College	

Evidently the province considered these works such a success, it continued them: after 1930, there were:

Parishes	*Colleges*	*High Schools*	*Retreat Houses*
7 parishes	Loyola University	Jesuit Dallas	Manresa
	Spring Hill College	Jesuit El Paso	Our Lady of the Oaks
		Jesuit New Orleans	Montserrat
		Jesuit Houston	Ignatius House
		Jesuit Shreveport	Xavier Hall
		Jesuit Tampa	

Other apostolic works were in time accepted, such as Corpus Christi Minor Seminary in Texas; still others grew out of its ranks, such as the Mission Band. Moreover, the New Orleans Province was entrusted with a mission to Ceylon/Sri Lanka which lasted from 20th century until the end of its colonial period. In addition, members of the province worked with the poor at the *Centro Kennedy* in Campinas, Brazil. Some Jesuits served in the Jesuit province in Paraguay. Individual Jesuits wound up in Russia, the Caroline Islands, Zambia and Zimbabwe. The crest of the wave came in 1965 when the population of Jesuits in the province crested at 634. This is as far as the wave stretched, after which it steadily receded.

How did this affect the Brothers in the Province? At first, very little. Brothers were always the pillars of the parishes and schools which the province operated. But changes began in the 1950s when Brothers such as Lloyd Barry called for a clarification of the identity of the Brother and thus an evaluation in the best use of them. Both aims were in the making, as we saw in the introduction of this book. Brothers were identified, like the priests, as full and equal Jesuits. This had the added effect that the jobs and tasks to which the brothers would be assigned should utilize the talent of the individual brother. Thus Brothers were to be taught to read and write, and those with some clerical or mechanical skill were to attain a college degree. Brothers, moreover, were to be encouraged to take the same course of studies as the scholastics, including earning a degree in theology, so as to teach and to give retreats. Thus on July 31, 2014, when the New Orleans and Missouri provinces merged into the USA Central and Southern Province, the Brothers, whose lives we are following, had among them a PhD, MBA, MDiv, several BA's, as well as numerous professional licenses for skills such as refrigeration, electricity, and maintenance. Brothers, moreover, were treasurers of the province, house ministers, house consultors and province consultors.

Br. Manuel Arrizabalaga, SJ
1879 – 1965

Manuel Arrizabalaga Olaizola was born in 1879 in the Basque country near where St. Ignatius was raised. He entered the Novitiate at San Sebastian, Spain in 1897. From the beginning he demonstrated distinctive culinary talent. So, when the theologate at Oña needed a cook, Manuel was sent to them, where he completed his Novitiate. In 1902 Manuel volunteered to work in America and took the steamer to the United States.

He was assigned as the cook of the Novitiate in Macon, Ga (1903-04). He then moved to Loyola University in New Orleans in the same capacity and worked for nearly a decade (1904-14). After the great hurricane, Manuel went to Galveston, Texas to assist in the reconstruction of St. Mary's College (1914-19). He returned East to Spring Hill College in Mobile, Ala as manager of the kitchen (1919-21), a job he also performed at Jesuit High in Shreveport, La (1921-23). "Go West" he did, first as cook for the Immaculate Conception Parish in Albuquerque, New Mexico (1923-26) and then for the Church of the Holy Family (1926-29). He returned to Spring Hill College in the capacity of horticulturist (1929-30). He was attached to the Missouri Province for five years: one year in St. Louis and four at St. Marys in Kansas(1931-35).

In time he settled on Brother "ABC" as his name because he failed to get his American brothers to say "Arrizabalaga." He vigorously supported Franco in the Spanish Civil War, signaling this by banging his cane on the floor at news of Franco's success. But it was the children who were his main work and in their "grown-up" memories he is still alive.

Manuel eventually came to Grand Coteau, La as the groundskeeper (1936-42). Shortly after, he was posted to El Paso, Texas where he served in three different Jesuit establishments: his chief work as cook for the House of Writers (1942-44), then as the parish's receptionist (1944-46), and as sacristan. He returned as cook for two years at the House of Writers (1948-50). He went back to Sacred Heart Church, this time in retirement (1950-54). Finally, Brother ABC was sent to Grand Coteau because of poor health, but he lived another eleven years as the groundskeeper (1954-65).

On his second day of "retirement" he got a hoe to prepare a playing field for the local children and from that day, all of his efforts were for them. He sold marbles to make money to buy basketballs. He begged old bats and torn balls from the novices and juniors and repaired them for further service. Truly he suffered the little ones to come to him. He celebrated his diamond jubilee in the Society on July 25, 1957. Manuel Arrizabalaga, SJ died of a heart attack on December 13, 1965 at the age of 86 and 68 as a

Jesuit. His obituary read: "The New Orleans Province was deprived of the earthly presence of one of its truly unique religious. With no fanfare and as quietly as he had lived his dedicated sixty-eight years of service, Brother ABC passed to his eternal reward."

Br. Lloyd A. Barry, SJ
1913 – 2002

Lloyd Barry was born on June 15, 1913. He earned a degree in mechanical engineering from Louisiana State University in 1941, after which on December 23, 1941, he joined the Order as a Brother, which gave him distinctive professional status in the province. He publicly urged that all Jesuit Brothers receive appropriate education according to their abilities and the Order's needs. Lloyd was assigned to various high schools and parishes in the province (Grand Coteau, La, fourteen years; Spring Hill in Mobile, Ala, ten; Jesuit High in Dallas, Texas, fifteen; Sacred Heart Parish, El Paso, Texas, seven). Beginning in 1960, he supervised the projects and works of the "Brothers' Maintenance Corps."

Lloyd wrote once that "I didn't set out to be a 'teacher'" and "I have never taught a class," but he, in fact, taught many classes to Jesuit Brothers. It was not enough that he was a recognized leader who shared his knowledge and skills with the Jesuit Brothers. In 1957 he returned to Grand Coteau to take charge of the Brothers' Technical Training Program, whose aim was to ensure that each Brother receive appropriate training, status and respect in the Society. He remarked on the occasion of the final vows of Brother Charles Doherty: "Through the dedication to God of his prayers, works, and sacrifices, he will share in all the rights, privileges and obligations of all the members of the Order." Brothers are Jesuits!

One of Lloyd's greatest contributions was his effort to inform people of the vocation of the Jesuit Brother. "What is a Jesuit brother? He is the man who teaches art at Spring Hill. … Before any of these he is a JESUIT in the full sense of the word. The motivation in all JESUITS is the same: 'For the greater glory of God and for the Salvation of Souls.' … Their basic spiritual training is the same … Their community exercises are the same."

Vatican II urged religious orders to return to their sources. In his investigation of the history of the Brothers in the Society of Jesus, Lloyd found that in the early Society there was no separation of classes, although Rule 14 prohibited brothers from learning, if illiterate, when they entered the order. But he found in Ignatius' writings three things about the first Brothers: 1) juridical equality, 2) religious identity in the full sense, and 3) commitment to serve the Society in those things in which others cannot engage without detriment to the common good. Two Fathers General in the twentieth century affirmed what Lloyd was laboring for. Wladimir Ledochowski said: "Brothers should have quality education and training;" Jean-Baptiste Janssens remarked : "We have only one 'social class,' that of the sons of the same society."

Two periods of his life illustrate a directly pastoral bent. In 1965 he was posted to Campinas, Brazil. From 1970 to 1973 he joined Brothers of the New Orleans Province, already there, Tony Coco and Bob Hollingsworth, at *Centro Kennedy*, a Jesuit vocational school, trying to teach the un-employed a trade. From 1988 to 1995 he was stationed at Sacred Heart in El Paso, where he found scope to engage in direct ministry to the poor and needy.

Lloyd was a champion who fought constantly for the Province to make the most and best use of Jesuit Brothers, which meant both appropriate education and training and an elevation of the level of respect and status of a Jesuit Brother. Br. Lloyd A. Barry SJ died minutes after sunrise on Easter Sunday March 31, 2002, God's exclamation point on a rich and zealous life. He was 88 years old and 61 years a Jesuit.

Br. Noel Bellemin, SJ
1866 – 1943

Noel Bellemin was born in Novalese, Savoie on July 1, 1866 of Francois and Francoise Bellemin. He was schooled in the same town, and upon completing of school he worked as a clerk. He entered the Order in Macon, Ga on February 18, 1914, taking his first vows in March 14, 1916. His signature ministry was as refectorian in six successive communities in the Province. He remained at Macon from 1914 until 1921, when he moved up the road to Augusta, Ga (1921-24). He moved south and west, first to Loyola University in New Orleans and then to Spring Hill College in Mobile, Ala. He made a cameo appearance in Shreveport, La (1924-25), after which he was posted to Grand Coteau, La (1925-39), where he took his final vows in 1925. We do not know anything more about him, except to note that Brother Noel Bellemin, SJ died on July 29, 1943.

Br. Louis J. Bethancourt, SJ
1875 – 1952

Louis J. Bethancourt, a native of Bonnet Carré, La, was born on July 26, 1875. He entered the Order on December 12, 1905 in Macon, Ga, where he did his Novitiate. He remained there for five years, assigned as the refectorian for the large community. He was also available for whatever task or job which needed to be done. He spent one year at the College in Galveston, Texas, performing different tasks, such as carpentry and iron working (1913-14). When he was assigned to Loyola University in New Orleans, he wore many hats: refectorian, monitor of the furnace, sacristan, and the person in charge of clothing supplies (1914-20). He returned to Macon for two years, basically continuing the same tasks (1920-22). Br. Louis was next assigned to Spring Hill College in Mobile, Ala, where he labored for the next 29 years (1922-51), in a variety of jobs: carpenter and monitor of the furnace, and new tasks such as electrician, maintenance, and any other tasks that needed to be done. We might deduce from this sketch of him that he was talented and respected for his labors and that, unlike most other Jesuits, he remained in the same place for an extended time, clearly a sign that he was a good Jesuit to live with. Br. Louis Bethancourt retired to Grand Coteau, where he died on July 3, 1952 at the age of 77, and a Jesuit Brother for 47 years.

Br. Ferrell Blank, SJ
1935 – 20??

Ferrell was born on December 18, 1935 in Gramecy, La. Fortunately he never lost his native country accent. As a young man he had a strong association with Fr. Michael Majoli at Manresa Retreat House in Convent, La; but even when invited to eat with the Jesuits of the Manresa community, no one talked to him about "Jesuit Brothers." Nevertheless he entered the Order on March 27, 1956, as a Brother novice. He began immediately to learn the many crafts and skills which eventually distinguished his service. His "college" consisted of a series of training programs, especially the ICS in maintenance; he became a carpenter, plumber and a reader of blueprints. He trained in refrigeration maintenance, and was inducted into the "Refrigeration Service Engineer Society" in 1975. Immediately after this, he became certified as a plant engineer #120 (1977).

Ferrell has spent most of his life at Spring Hill College in Mobile, Ala, with a few brief exceptions in Atlanta, Ga; Loyola in New Orleans; and Houston, Texas. Everywhere he lived, Ferrell was well liked by his Jesuit associates and neighbors and colleagues. He was indeed "Frugal Ferrell," for he seemed incapable of discarding anything, which led to closets and rooms filled with stuff. People who know Ferrell like him and consider him friendly, helpful, reliable and charitable. In addition to all of his other crafts, he served as Spring Hill's locksmith. He made it a point to make his annual retreat with other Jesuits. In 2005 President Greg Lucey honored him for his 50 years of service at the Hill. And he is greatly praised for his excellent maintenance of Arrupe Villa on Perdido Bay, Ala, where he spends half of his time as its custodian. He is involved in the Coast Guard Auxiliary, the Knights of Columbus, and most recently he is a member of "The Men of St. Joseph," a lay spiritual organization.

Br. John Blenke, SJ
1883 – 1946

John Blenke was born in Weerslo, the Netherlands on June 24, 1883. He emigrated to the United States and entered the Novitiate in Macon, Ga on September 2, 1914. After his formation, he remained in Macon six years, primarily as carpenter but also as cook (1916-22). He was moved to Loyola in New Orleans with expanded responsibilities; he added iron-working to his carpentry and became the custodian of the heating system for twenty-four years (1922-46). He was assigned other small jobs, such as assisting in the library and serving as sacristan. Br. John Blenke, SJ died on September 10, 1946; he was 63 years old and 32 as a Jesuit Brother.

Br. Charles J. Blouin, SJ
1925 – 2009

Charlie was born in Gonzales, La on April 12, 1925, in the shadow of the Manresa House of Retreats. He was educated locally, but when he became part of the US Army he learned first hand what can't be found in books. It is a miracle that he survived all of the campaigns that he fought in, especially the Italian campaign. And it is no surprise that the Army honored him and weighed him down with the following medals: Victory Medal, Good Conduct Medal, European-African-Middle Eastern Campaign and three Bronze Stars. But Charlie was not through with the Service, for when discharged by the Army, he enlisted in the US Navy in which he served four years. He was honorably discharged on April 11, 1960.

He joined another kind of army on June 1, 1962. After his spiritual boot camp, Charlie stayed at St. Charles College in Grand Coteau, La as assistant treasurer for two years (1964-66). He then became the treasurer for the high school in Shreveport, La for three years (1966-69). He returned to Grand Coteau and the year after that, he was sent to Shreveport. He traveled to Jesuit High in Tampa, Fla to be its minister (1971-73). He returned to Grand Coteau, but this time as house manager for Our Lady of the Oaks Retreat House (1973-75). He was one year at Spring Hill College in Mobile, Ala before being posted for three years at Jesuit High in New Orleans (1976-79). He was sent back as minister at the Oaks for one year and three years as minister at St. Charles College (1979-83). Since Charlie had not been stationed in Houston yet, he was sent to Strake Jesuit High for two years. Nothing would do but to send him clear across the province from Houston back to Tampa and to his old job as minister (1985-92). He moved one more time, to Loyola in New Orleans, where he served ten years as the community treasurer. He eventually was retired to Ignatius Residence because of dementia. Br. Charles J. Blouin, SJ died on August 10, 2009; he was 84 years old and 49 years a Jesuit Brother.

Brs. Bob Hollingsworth
and Charlie Blouin

Br. Everard Joseph Booth, SJ
1917 – 1986

Everard, known to his friends as "Tooty," was born in Morgan City, La on August 20, 1917. His education took place wherever the family lived, first New Orleans, then Vicksburg, Ms and back to New Orleans. Although in 1934 he graduated from a high school named for a young Jesuit saint (St. Aloysius), he did not escape the pull of the Jesuits in New Orleans. Immediately that summer he entered the Order in Grand Coteau, La as a postulant brother on July 30, 1934. After vows, he remained at Grand Coteau for six years as buyer, assistant bursar, assistant infirmarian, person in charge of the poultry yard and guest refectorian. From this boot camp, he emerged with skill as buyer and bursar. He joined the staff of the provincial's office as associate socius and assistant province procurator (1941-46). Tooty was in the vanguard of Jesuits from the New Orleans province who became part of the mission to Ceylon, which had been entrusted to the Province. He spent his first year there at St. Michael's College in Batticaloa. When it was obvious that the Ceylon mission needed printing facilities, he traveled to De Nobili Press in Maduri, India to learn this trade (1947). Back at St. Michael's he undertook for seven years many old jobs: bursar, buyer, bookstore manager (1947-54). Because of illness, he returned to America for treatment. After six months he was back in Ceylon, now at St. Joseph's college in Trincomalee, serving in diverse clerical capacities (1955-60). He returned permanently to the Province, being assigned to St. Charles College in Grand Coteau, La (1960-61). Then began his long tenure in the Seminary and Mission Bureau as the office manager (1961-71). During this period he joined the Knights of Columbus, achieving the status of Past Grand Knight. Finally he could claim to be a Blue Jay, a graduate of the high school in New Orleans, when he was assigned there in two capacities, prefect of discipline and manager of its bookstore (1971-84). It was eminently wise to make this friendly and cordial man the director of alumni. His health was good for his age, but in a fog of confusion, he was killed in a head-on collision on February 23, 1986. Br. Everard Joseph Booth, SJ was 68 years old at his death and 52 years a Jesuit. Few Jesuits have been mourned as "Tooty" was.

Br. Richard Herrick Bray, SJ
1903 – 1972

Richard Herrick Bray was born in New Orleans on Sept. 28, 1903. Since his own name, Herrick, was a curiosity, it helps to know that his parents were elegantly named: Cornelius Charles Bray and Eleanora Herrick Bray. Richard's health was so poor that all his schooling was done at home. Like Richard himself, there is a lacuna in his file about any other details of his life. He himself was a very humble, self-effacing person, which may account for the absence of information about him in the Order's files. For sure, Richard began postulancy as a Brother in Grand Coteau, La on May 27, 1956, and took his vows on July 2, 1958. His life consisted of three apostolic appointments: first sacristan of the Church of the Immaculate Conception in New Orleans (August 1958 to August 1963) and porter at the Jesuit House of Studies in Mobile, Ala (1963-1967). Third, he returned to St. Charles College in April 1967 to serve as porter for five years. Because he entered the order at the age of 55, he was already old by many standards, and never enjoyed good health. If not calling attention to oneself was a virtue, Br. Bray achieved his sainthood in this manner. Although full of eccentricities, he was friendly, entertaining (whether he wished to be so or not), and observably pious. Brother Richard Herrick Bray, SJ, died at St. Charles College in Grand Coteau on December 12, 1972, at the age of sixty-nine.

Br. William N. Bryan, SJ
1902 – 1969

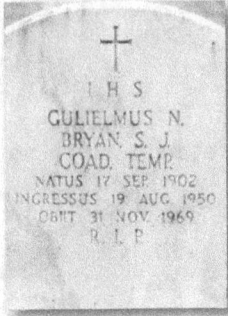

William Bryan was born in the heart of Evangeline territory, St. Martinville, La on September 17, 1902. He was in his late forties when he entered the Novitiate not far from his birthplace at Grand Coteau on August 19, 1950. After his vows, he remained at Grand Coteau learning to operate the laundry of the college, and serving as associate to the team renovating St. Charles College. When time for his tertianship came, he traveled to El Paso, Texas for this probation (1959-60) and remained at the high school for four years as assistant refectorian and assistant at the Lord's Ranch, a facility for troubled youth (1960-64). He moved to the high school in Tampa, Fla as sacristan to both the school's and community's chapels and to serve as refectorian (1964-68). Bill was aging and failing, and so he returned to Grand Coteau to retire and "pray for the Society." Br. William N. Bryan, SJ died on November 31, 1969 at the age of 67 and 19 as a Jesuit Brother.

Br. Halcott T. Burges, SJ
1875 – 1968

Harry was born in Alexandria, La on September 25, 1875. Fifty years later he entered the Order at Grand Coteau, La on July 4, 1925. Like most Brothers, Harry performed many different jobs and was posted to many houses. For three years after the Novitiate, he remained in Grand Coteau as infirmarian of the community. He was sent to Loyola University in New Orleans where he apprenticed as a carpenter and worker in metal and then became the community's cook (1930-34). He returned to Grand Coteau to resume his job as infirmarian and to practice his building skills (1934-37). Back in New Orleans, he was the refectorian and chief of the kitchen (1937-39). He moved to downtown New Orleans and the Immaculate Conception Church where he worked for sixteen years as sacristan and prefect of the altar boys (1939-55). He picked up other jobs such as house buyer and infirmarian, which he did for many years there. Harry was now seventy-five years old and so the Province retired him to Grand Coteau where his only task was assistant infirmarian (1957-68). Harry nearly exterminated the blue jays on the property by trapping them and removing them from the ranks of predator birds; no amount of pleas from Jesuit High Blue Jay Jesuits could persuade him to stop. Halcott T. Burges, SJ, died on October 17, 1968 at the age of 93 and 43 years as a Jesuit Brother.

Br. Manuel Cabral, SJ
1933 – 2008

Manny Cabral was born in Durango, Mexico on April 7, 1933. His family moved to El Paso, Texas early enough for him to receive all of his schooling there. In 1952, the year that he graduated from high school, he entered the Order in Grand Coteau, La on July 30, 1952 as a Jesuit Brother. After his formation, he remained in Grand Coteau for three years and then began his labors throughout the province. He was a naturally outgoing man, who became the assistant to the introvert Br. Michael

Moore, who rarely spoke a word. Moreover, Manny had a bit of the clown in him, as evidenced by his climb to the top of the water tower to do maintenance, after which he climbed even higher to do a hand-stand on the very top of the structure. He joined the maintenance corps of Brothers at the House of Studies in Mobile, Ala for five years (1958-63). He was then posted to the newly opened high school in El Paso for two years (1963-65), after which he became the sacristan at St. John's in Shreveport, La (1965-67). Manny joined the Jesuit Brothers' Work Corps 1967-71, doing renovations on various buildings belonging to the province's institutions. He remained in New Orleans to work in the Office of Development and Alumni at Loyola (1971-74). He then returned to Grand Coteau for two years before moving West for the remainder of his Jesuit life. He was assigned to Sacred Heart Church in El Paso for one year, then to the high school in Houston for three years (1977-80). He was granted a leave of absence from the ministries of the province (1980-85), but returned to his duties at the Immaculate Conception Church in Albuquerque, New Mexico (1985-94), where he was employed at a local TV station. In 1994 he was reassigned to Sacred Heart Church for the rest of his Jesuit life. Manuel Cabral, SJ died on July 22, 2008; he was 75 years old and 56 a Jesuit Brother.

Br. Anthony Coco, SJ
1929 – 20??

Between 1880 and 1920, over three million Sicilians migrated to the USA, among them Tony's grandfather. From New Orleans, he traveled to a colony of Sicilians in Helena, Arkansas. In 1904 Tony's father, Rosario, and his uncle, Charles, arrived in New York and went to Helena because of a marriage between Rosario and Tony's mother, which was already arranged in Sicily. "The custom," Tony said, "proved successful and produced a happy and fruitful union." Tony was born on May 11, 1929, one of eleven children.

As soon as Tony could hold a wrench, he began taking things apart and putting them back together, eventually working in Clyde Smith's garage at the age of ten. Mr. Smith put him on the payroll at full salary when eleven. By twelve he was an iconic figure in the automobile world, acknowledged by no less than John Hix's 1942 newspaper section, *Strange as it seems*. "I was," as Tony said, "the youngest salaried mechanic in America."

Although he missed the draft of WWII, he wound up atop the draft list when the Korean war broke out. Even the Army recognized his mechanical skills, and so trained him to repair tanks disabled on the battle field. "Fine by me," said Tony, because "One tank model was powered by two Cadillac engines and had hydraulic transmissions." Both before and after the war, Tony worked for various automotive dealerships, but he always found them disappointing. The magnetism of the Jesuits kept pulling him, with the result that he entered the Novitiate at Grand Coteau, La on July 10, 1957. After vows, he was assigned the rebuilding of an army-surplus bulldozer: he took it apart, cleaned every single piece, and re-assembled it. With one turn of the key it started. Tony wasn't surprised at all. He was posted to the Jesuit House of Studies in Mobile, Ala in charge of maintenance, learning as he went plumbing, electrical engineering and air conditioning.

When the call went out for Jesuits to work in Brazil, Tony volunteered (he apparently learned nothing in the Army). And in 1966, he was sent with Br. Bob Hollingsworth, an expert in concrete, to Campinas, in the state of São Paulo. Here he belonged to a mobile Brothers' Work Team, which operated out of a van which was a rolling shop. Besides repairing anything metal and electric, he helped people build houses by providing skills in carpentry, plumbing and electricity. Eventually, Fr. Harold Rahm, SJ arranged for the purchase of an abandoned orphanage, which was to become the *Centro Presidente John Kennedy*. A most valuable tool for these people was the sewing machine; Tony asked Singer Sewing Machine Company for five machines, but got none; yet, there were good machines at hand, except that they were pedal driven. How could his people work them unless Tony could help; so, he apprenticed with the quality control supervisor at Singer. Success was such that he became an "ambulatory technician," going to the houses with broken machines, not only repairing them, but not charging them with punishing fees.

With the exception of an occasional year back in America, Tony remained in Brazil. Yet his job matured. For nine years (1966-75) he fulfilled the task of "technical assistance to the poor" at *Centro Kennedy* in Campinas. For the next two years, he labored at the same task in Itaici, Indaiatuba. He returned to Campinas in the state of São Paulo and from 1977 until 2002 he was the Assistant Director of the Center there. After one year back in the province (2003), he returned to being Assistant Director of Centro Kennedy in Campinas.

He finally returned to Ignatius Residence in New Orleans in charge of maintenance (2005-2013), and when that community moved to St. Charles College in May of 2013, he came as well, doing all things and being especially skilled now in the hardware of computers.

So many years spent in Brazil in technical assistance to the poor, yet the record of these is so facilely expressed in one sentence. Who is this Br. Coco? Obviously a man of immense generosity and constancy. At his Jubilee in 2007, he wrote:

> The years in Brazil were wonderful years during which I learned the ways and language
> of a new culture. There were periods of frustration with issues involving governmental
> bureaucracy. However there were many more times of great joy as I met the person of
> Christ in the needs and the poverty of the people there. I am most grateful to God for the
> opportunities I had to serve and to work among the wonderful people of Brazil.

We also know him as the president of the fan club of his brother, Frank Coco, SJ, the jazz clarinetist. And if you want to find him, just listen for soft singing or humming in the house; music is as frequent on his lips as words.

Br. Raymond Cody, SJ
1905 – 1974

Raymond John Cody was born in Minneapolis, Minn on January 23, 1905. After graduating from Spring Hill College, in Mobile, Ala, he immediately entered the Society on August 14, 1924. He studied philosophy, taught in Tampa, Fla, New Orleans and Shreveport, La, then studied theology in St. Marys, Ks. His Jesuit priesthood preparation was complete but for one thing. In his third year of theology, he decided against being ordained. He was sent to tertianship in the hope that he would change his mind. Eventually *Brother* Cody was sent to Florissant, Mo to begin his Novitiate as a Jesuit Brother. The following is an excerpt from his letter to Father Provincial (January 2, 1945):

I am convinced that I should not go on to the priesthood, to priestly work, but rather ask to spend the rest of my life in the Society as a temporal coadjutor (Brother). … To me the brother's life holds no special attraction, naturally speaking. What appeals to me in the lay brotherhood of the Society is religious life in the Society, the life that I have been living happily for the past twenty years.

Because of his education, Ray went to Rome to be the Brother Secretary to the American Assistant. He returned to New Orleans to serve as the Brother Socius to many Fathers Provincial (1946-69), and became indispensable to the province. His peers nicknamed the humorous Ray as "Lew," after a popular comedian of the 20's.

Many generations of Jesuits had dealings with Ray because of his lengthy stint as Socius to the Provincial. He read most of the incoming letters and typed the replies. No one ever spoke critically of him or his work. All of us were spoken to or written to with respect, to which we responded in kind.

The last years of his life became difficult because of Ray's declining health and memory. At one point the province decided to hire lay typists, which meant nudging Ray from his signature job as socius. His perfectionism, which had earlier served him well, later became concrete into which his ways were set. But his worst fear was to become useless, so he took on numerous minor jobs, such as three trips daily to the post office and refectory chores, such as cleaning up breakfast dishes, setting the supper table, serving coffee and later doing the supper dishes. His new mode of serving included giving rides to neighbors waiting for the bus, chatting up the kids in the neighborhood; they responded by waving to him on his trips and even brought him flowers. They always wanted to tell him how their school play went.

"Raymond John Cody, SJ" said Tom Clancy, SJ, "had all the virtues of an old-fashioned Jesuit." "Lew" died on December 24, 1974 at the age of 69; he was 50 years a Jesuit. In Tom Clancy's obit we read, "Many Jesuits to whom I owed a great deal are dead, but I don't remember any Jesuit death affecting me as much as Lew's (Ray's)."

Br. Leo J. Collison, SJ
1902 – 1975

Leo was born in Philadelphia, Pa on April 9, 1902. Sometime during the period before he entered the Order, Leo was a hotel manager. At forty-four years old, he entered the Jesuit Novitiate in Grand Coteau, La on May 9, 1946. Leo remained at Grand Coteau for two more years as the infirmarian (1948-50); he spent one year at Manresa Retreat House in Convent, La as infirmarian, sacristan and assistant house manager. He moved to New Orleans, first spending three years at Loyola as refectorian and sacristan (1951-54) and then six years at Jesuit High School as sacristan, the person in charge of clothing supplies, and receptionist (1955-62). He was then posted to Jesuit High in Dallas, Texas for fourteen years, or, for the rest of his life (1962-75). His tasks were more or less the same as previously mentioned: sometimes refectorian, sometimes sacristan, and always available as the community's maintenance man. Br. Leo J. Collison, SJ died on January 10, 1975 in Dallas; he was 72 years old and 28 as a Jesuit Brother.

Br. John A. Cunningham, SJ
1908 – 1972

John was one of the many Irish who immigrated to America and who discerned a vocation to be a Jesuit Brother. Although John was born in Benraw, Ireland on September 28, 1908, he waited until he was forty years old to enter the Novitiate at Grand Coteau, La on May 13, 1950. After vows, he remained two years at Grand Coteau as refectorian and caretaker of the wine cellar. He was then missioned to Holy Name of Jesus Church in New Orleans for sixteen years, which proved to be the rest of his life (1954-71). John's two jobs there were both part of the church's ministry: sacristan and associate moderator of the Society of St. John Berchmans. And he was always available for any task that needed doing. Toward the end of his life, even as his health was failing, he persuaded his superiors to let him visit Ireland. Shortly after his pilgrimage began Br. John A. Cunningham, SJ died in Leitrim, Ireland on May 28, 1972 at the age of 64 and 22 as a Jesuit Brother.

Br. William J. Dardis, SJ
1940 – 20??

William J. Dardis was born on May 11, 1940, the eldest of four boys; he had one sister with whom he has been very close. After a traditional Catholic education, he graduated from Jesuit High New Orleans in 1958; his brothers all followed him to Jesuit, partly because their uncle, Father Joe Dardis, SJ, served as magnet. Billy immediately entered the Novitiate on Aug 14, 1958 as a scholastic novice, but after seven months transferred to the grade of temporal coadjutor (Brother). He was on the crest of the wave which urged formal, even collegiate, training, as urged by Ignatius Fabacher, SJ and Lloyd Barry, SJ. Hence Billy took math and history classes in the Juniorate and then attended the training program in Milford, Ohio where he studied building maintenance, and then went for similar studies to Ohio Mechanics Institute. In 1968 he attended night school at Loyola University New Orleans, earning a Business degree in 1973.

He returned to Jesuit High New Orleans where, with the exception of one year, he has served until the present. His ministry breaks into distinctive parts. From 1964 until 1969 he was the assistant in charge of boiler maintenance and electricity. In 1967 he was appointed the sub-minister for ordinary affairs and the next year he became the community's postman. The next block of his ministry was focused on the maintenance of the Jesuit High complex (1970 - 1982). During this time, he served as the minister for community affairs (1974) and he began teaching theology in the school (1972). In 1973 he was designated a House Consultor, a position of importance and insight; he remained a consultor from 1973 until 1982. In 1983 he went to Marquette University to learn about public relations.

Brs. Larry Lundin and Billy Dardis

Upon his return in 1984, he served as the associate director of alumni and book keeper. He was reappointed a House Consultor, serving from 1986 until the present day. He was promoted to director of alumni affairs in 1990 and served there until 2004. He was made

the minister of the Jesuit community in 1997, a service he continued until 2012. In 1994, Billy returned to the classroom as a teacher of theology. In 2005 he was made director of special projects, a task he has continued to the present day. So much for his time line and assignment roster.

Billy Dardis glows like a light bulb when he talks about his life at this time. He has a good sense of humor, evidenced by his call to an electrician for help, which electrician said to an associate: "Go over there; that boy's going to electrocute himself." He laughs often and easily. The fact that he has been appointed so often to positions which require maturity and smarts, one would say that he is a solid man, whose judgment one wants to hear. His service has been recognized by the school, first for 20 years of service as Alumni Director and then as Director of Special Projects.

We know the major parts of his ministry, but equally important for appreciating Billy are the extras he did, such as driving students wherever needed: to retreats, to cheerleader practice, etc. He enjoyed the boys and showed this as director of the bookstore for fifteen years. Rare was the school event which he did not attend. Not only did he drive the Sodality to Mobile, Ala for their retreat, he stayed and cooked for them. At times he served as tutor to Jesuit students in math, science and Latin.

A man's hobbies tell us much about him. Billy cultivates Christmas trees on a plantation in Picayune, Ms; when possible he is there every week. And fishing. He promoted the annual Jesuit fishing rodeo with such success, that he was officially recognized as "A Legend of the Fishing Rodeo" in 2015. Billy is remarkable in the Province for remaining so long in the same community; he claims that he told the Provincial "It does not matter what I do here, so long as I stay here." As Billy talked to me, I was stunned by how happy he is and has been; he loves being with students and alumni, which is the best gospel he can preach to them. He concluded by telling me that he is convinced that he has had the "hundredfold" promised by Jesus, that is, he is electrified by all the families he knows and the friendships he enjoys. "A hundredfold" already.

Br. Charles Robert Doherty, SJ
1930 – 2007

Bob was born in Byers, Texas on December 17, 1930. He entered the Society at Grand Coteau, La on March 26, 1957. On the occasion of the jubilee feast celebrating his 50 years as a Jesuit, he wrote a modest summary of his vocation which is the best record we have of his life.

> In my parish in Denver I heard about the great work of Father Harold Rahm in El Paso with the poor. So when I got a job in that city, I joined him at Our Lady's Youth Center after working hours. He needed help with the sports program and that's where I helped.

Bob said that Harold Rahm wanted more from him and encouraged him to join the Jesuits.

Bob worked in maintenance in various schools most of his Jesuit career. Equally interesting was his multifaceted outreach to students in our schools and to a variety of other young people. He gave much time to the Knights of Columbus, to alcohol abuse counseling, to various spiritual programs, and even as a volunteer at the Aquarium of the Americas in New Orleans. His pleasant and friendly disposition was a significant tool for his apostolate. After many hard years of work, he was assigned as assistant director at Ignatius Residence. As the years passed, so did his mind. Charles Robert Doherty, SJ died on November 21, 2007, 76 years old and 50 as a Jesuit Brother.

Br. Henry Thomas Donellan, SJ
1917 – 1992

Henry Thomas Donellan was born in Bogalousa, La on October 8, 1917. He was, however, rescued from there and educated in Baton Rouge, first in a public school (1924-28) and then at Sacred Heart Primary School (1928-32) and at Catholic High School (1932-36). After a year on his own, he began his Postulancy as a Jesuit Brother on February 27, 1937, taking his first vows on September 8, 1939. His signature ministry was that of Sacristan, which he performed throughout his apostolic life, with a brief exception. His first assignment was to the Gesú in Miami, Fla (1940-43), after which he served in the same capacity at Holy Name of Jesus Church in New Orleans (1943-45). He moved downtown in New Orleans to the Immaculate Conception Church (1945-47). During this year he made his Tertianship at Grand Coteau, La, taking his final vows on February 2, 1948. Since he was already at Grand Coteau, he remained there 1947-48. But next year he was back at the Immaculate Conception in New Orleans (1948-56), so he was known to all the Jesuit High altar boys who served downtown. For a change, he was assigned to Jesuit High School New Orleans as refectorian and porter (1956-59), reverting back to his speciality, sacristan at the high school. Then Henry settled down as sacristan of Holy Name of Jesus from 1963-85, becoming Sacristan of the Rectory chapel for three years. He became the "utility" brother at the rectory in 1988 and remained there for the rest of his life. Except for three years in Miami, Henry live the rest of his entire life in Louisiana, from Baton Rouge to New Orleans. A lucky man?

Henry Thomas Donellan, SJ died on November 5, 1992, at the age of 75 and 55 years a Jesuit Brother.

Front Row: ????, Br. Keller, Fr. Bernard, Br. Blenke, Br. Bellermay
Back Row: Br. Frank Eaton, Br. Burchardt, Br. Mendizable

Br. Francis X. Eaton, SJ
1893 – 1942

Francis X. Eaton is another Irishman who was born in Dublin, Ireland on May 12, 1893 but who labored in the American South. Shortly after his arrival in America, he joined the Jesuits at the Novitiate in Macon, Ga on September 24, 1909. Initially he entered the Jesuits to be trained as a priest, but he quickly discerned that service as a Jesuit Brother was the true direction of his vocation. He remained in Macon for six more years, several years as the refectorian of the community, as the gardener of its produce and vegetables, and three years as its cook. He was on the road for several years, first at Spring Hill College in Mobile, Ala, where his labors shifted to carpentry and supervision of the heating system (1918-19), then at Galveston, Texas, where he returned to cooking and food production (1919-20), then to Shreveport, La, where his tasks in Galveston were continued (1920-21), and then to Grand Coteau, La to add carpentry to his skill set (1921-22). He returned to Galveston with a host of jobs: carpenter, sacristan, receptionist and refectorian (1922-24). After two years back at Shreveport doing the same jobs, he spent six years at Loyola University as refectorian, carpenter and buyer (1926-32). He was then posted to Grand Coteau for six years as baker (1932-38). He next moved to Jesuit High School in New Orleans for two years as sacristan and supervisor of the kitchen and dining room. He was the proverbial staff in the hand of the master. Francis was finally missioned to Jesuit High School in Tampa, Fla, his final assignment (1940-42). His burdens now became light: he was the director of the altar boys ("Knights of the Altar") and sacristan. On November 21, 1942 Br. Francis X. Eaton, SJ died in Tampa at the age of 49 years and 33 as a Jesuit Brother.

Br. Joseph S. Eaton, SJ
1892 – 1950

On May 7, 1892, Joseph S. Eaton was born in Rathgar, Ireland. The next news we have about him is his entry into the Novitiate in Macon, Ga on September 24, 1909, a very young man. His stated vocation in the Society was that of a priest, and so he spent the first five years of his vowed life in scholastic pursuits. Something was in flux, for the record indicates that in 1916, Joseph stopped his academic training and served as the Novitiate's "jack-of-all-trades" for two years. His first year as a Jesuit Brother was spent at Loyola University in New Orleans (1918-19) with light duties. He was then moved to Grand Coteau, La for three years, during which his duties remained light, namely, the person in charge of the common closet and clothing (1919-22). In 1922, he was posted to Spring Hill College in Mobile, Ala where he spent twenty-eight years, which was the rest of his life. He remained the custodian of clothing, both those of Jesuits and of the students. He began to serve as assistant infirmarian, often as receptionist and refectorian. He retired at Spring Hill College in 1949-50 to "Pray for the Society." On January 19, 1950, Br. Joseph S. Eaton, SJ died at the age of 58 and 41 as a Jesuit Brother. Because he was liked so much by his Jesuit peers, his death was deeply mourned.

Br. Walter A. Eckler, SJ
1929 – 20??

Walter was born on Sept. 30, 1929 in West Palm Beach, Fla. He remained in south Florida for twenty more years, being schooled at St. Ann Mission in West Palm Beach (1935-48). He spent 1948-49 in the US Naval Reserve and then a year at Palm Beach Junior College (1949). Then he entered the Novitiate on April 19, 1951. He typically experienced a variety of jobs in his first four years as a Jesuit:, in the bakery, laundry, shoe repair shop, and as tailor and as receptionist. Then from 1955 until 1961, he became sacristan, the groundskeeper, apprentice in the auto shop and on the farm.

Nothing in his background qualified him for his job as the manager of the St. Charles College farm and its cattle. From 1951 until 1974, Walter and a superior team of locals farmed the many acres of the college, harvesting sweet potatoes, corn and hay for the cattle, cotton for sale, and milk from a premier herd of dairy cows. It is so easy to write this, but Walter had to face droughts, hurricanes, machine failures, novices unused to farm labor, and all sorts of evil things which would spoil his day. It is no exaggeration to say that a third of the diet of the Jesuits at St. Charles College was produced under Walter's supervision. Never was there a skinny novice or junior. All this time he was also in charge of the farm vehicles which plowed, planted and harvested the acres of land belonging to the college. For four years (1965-69), he was also the supervisor of the College's fire department. Because he commanded the back-hoe, he became the man in charge of digging and filling the graves in the cemetery.

If nothing prepared him for the farm and cattle at Grand Coteau, nothing in his past qualified him to become the Dean of Students at Corpus Christi Minor Seminary in Corpus Christi, Texas (1974-79). He was in charge of discipline; and he regularly gave academic counseling to the students. Most importantly, he was a team player on the Jesuit staff and a unique icon to the students, a happy and holy Brother.

His next three assignments consisted of being the man in charge of maintenance for the following institutions. He served at Strake Jesuit College Prep in Houston (1979-82). From there he was transferred to Montserrat Retreat House in Lake Dallas, Texas (1982-86). And finally he took a giant leap West when he was assigned to the Catholic Mission in Koror, Palau (1986-89). Later he was assigned to St. Joseph Church in downtown Houston (1989-2003) as its minister and plant manager. After fourteen years, he was assigned to the Immaculate Conception Church in New Orleans as sacristan and assistant to the Director of the Parish Center (2003-09). Then he returned to Strake Jesuit in Houston as "house and grounds assistant."

Br. John Fillmore Elliot, SJ
1930 – 2004

J. Fillmore Elliot was born in New Orleans on December 31, 1930 of a spiritual family which produced two Jesuit priests (Clyde and Larion) and two Sisters of St. Joseph of Medaille. After graduation from Jesuit High, New Orleans, Fillmore joined the Jesuits in 1948.

Fillmore belonged to that generation of Jesuit Brothers who did not study for professional degrees. He "became" the community infirmarian for Grand Coteau and Spring Hill for more than twenty

years. His disposition was as therapeutic as any medicines he proffered. Was there ever a Jesuit so continually cheerful, extroverted and helpful by nature? He was notorious for adjusting the Society's rules for the care of the sick. If he had a failing, it would be that in his work he tended to run in all directions at the same time to do everything for everybody.

In 1974-77 he labored in Campinas, Brazil as nurse and sacristan. After Brazil, he undertook a similar ministry at the Immaculate Conception parish in Albuquerque, New Mexico (1978-84), in particular visiting the hospitals on a regular basis.

Fillmore suffered a near fatal heart attack in Albuquerque, so he was moved to the infirmary at Ignatius Residence in New Orleans. It came to light that beside serious cardiovascular problems, Fillmore suffered from diabetes. But as much as his health allowed, he spent seven years of ministry to the residents, driving some to their medical appointments and collecting their medicines. He helped the neighboring pastor with communion and other services. But he was not finished yet.

In 1993 he received certification in hospital pastoral ministry, which he then practiced in Tampa General Hospital in Florida for ten years, even when he was reduced to traveling by a motorized wheel chair. But his health required him to return to New Orleans for skilled nursing care at Our Lady of Wisdom Medical Center. In his final years he was renowned for making coffee for the people in his wing and bringing it to them first thing in the morning – quintessential Fillmore. And on Feb 24, 2004, just months before his death, Fillmore was crowned King of Mardi Gras at Our Lady of Wisdom Health Care Center. No one in the world could match his reign over chaos and mirth. His grade was that of Jesuit Brother, and J. Fillmore Elliot was also a brother to all Jesuits of the province. Br. John Fillmore Elliot, SJ died on June 26, 2004; he was 73 years old and 56 as a Jesuit Brother.

Br. John J. Emmett, SJ
1874 – 1951

John J. Emmett was born in Bradford, England on June 24, 1874. He was in his late fifties when he entered the Novitiate in Grand Coteau, La on December 18, 1931. He remained at Grand Coteau for sixteen years performing various tasks. First and foremost, he was the house tailor for the whole time he was there. As the resident cobbler, he kept the house shod. While at Grand Coteau, he served as sacristan of the Jesuit Church of St. Peter Claver for seven years (1935-42) and then at Christ the King Church. He is cited as an expert in the carving of the tombstones of Jesuits in the local cemetery (1941-49). He was also the college's storekeeper for four years. He labored for the last three years of his life at Xavier Hall, the province tertianship in Pass Christian, Ms, where his tasks diminished constantly (1949-51). Br. John J. Emmett SJ returned to New Orleans where he died on December 27, 1951 at the age of 77 years old and 21 as Jesuit Brother.

Br. Castenzio Ferlita, SJ
1938 – 20??

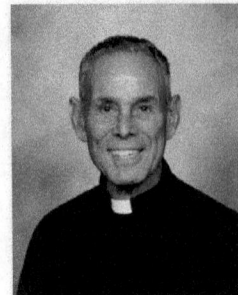

"Casey" Ferlita was born on Oct 15, 1938 in Tampa, Fla. On both sides, his parents were immigrants from Sicily, who were brought to Florida to plant orange trees. Hard working and poor, one grandfather told him "Work and get paid" but the other said "Work and get an education." After elementary education at Most Holy Name, he attended Tampa Jesuit and graduated in 1957. In his third year at Jesuit, although a starter on the football team, he was cut from basketball. But a nun at a local grade school snared him to coach basketball and softball at her school. A seed was surely planted. While at Jesuit, Charles Lashley, SJ attracted Casey as the first person to talk to him about a vocation, for he saw in Casey leadership. First a seed, and now a mentor. Casey spent two years in the Tampa National Guard as he attended three semesters at Tampa University. All the while he coached Junior High basketball and softball, as well as Junior Varsity football at Jesuit Tampa. His attempt at college proved unsuccessful, and he definitely did not wish to take over his father's ice cream business. His image of a religious Brother was revealed when he observed the Salesian Brothers at work in maintaining their institution. Now the vocation had some shape. He entered the Order on Aug 15, 1960 and began his spiritual formation as a Brother. After vows he remained at Grand Coteau in the Junior Brother Program. He trained to be an infirmarian (1964-65), a skill which he could call upon the rest of his life.

Casey belonged to the generation of Jesuit Brothers whose vocation was in flux. No longer did the Order desire that these men serve in obscurity. It was time to have them stand front and center. Moreover, Casey's generation was urged to get professional education, preferably in the area where their specialization would be utilized. Thus Casey pursued a degree in Health and Physical Education.

He was then assigned to Jesuit New Orleans as assistant athletic director and assistant prefect of discipline (1965-67), but he shed the discipline job in 1967 for that of school infirmarian as well as Coordinator of the Athletic Department (1967-71). As infirmarian he returned to Grand Coteau for two

years (1971-73). He earned a bachelors degree from Loyola University in New Orleans in 1975, concomitantly attending Houston Baptist University for specialized courses in sports paramedicine. Finally he was assigned to the job of athletic trainer and prefect of discipline at Strake Jesuit in Houston. This job lasted nearly forty years (1973 – 2010). During this time he became one of the public faces of the school, attending funerals and working with alumni, and counseling the students. He says that his service as disciplinarian as well as athletic trainer made him an apt person to teach the boys both discipline and control. When he turned 71, he downsized his commitment at Strake, becoming "assistant director" of athletic training, alumni and aide to the principal.

One is tempted to think of him as an idealist, but one of his favorite mottos is the one Br. Al Nowak, SJ told him; when Casey complained about this or that, Al shouted "You (Casey) live in heaven and we have to put up with this crap." A man's mentors and guides tell us much about that person; in his case, his mentors and guides are recognized Jesuits: Charles Lashley, SJ; Lloyd Barry, SJ; Johnny Edwards, SJ; and Charlie O'Neill, SJ. Casey always presented a cheerful face to the world. He is transparently good and, yes, holy. Goodness is eventually recognized and made public. Casey in 1987 received the "Tom Maddox Award as a 'Man for Others.'" And at a special social for alumni and parents, the school President, Brian Zinnamon, SJ, acknowledged and honored him for his service to the school and its students. He has always been focused in his assignments, especially anything to do with sports and training, for as he said, sports and training are his entree into the world of the students. He is what Jesuits call a "good community man," but because he lived basically at the high school in Houston, the other province institutions did not enjoy his presence. In the brochure for his celebration of being fifty years in the Society, he wrote: "I feel great gratitude to the Lord for my vocation as a Brother in the Society of Jesus, to my superiors, and to my Jesuit brethren. Also I am most grateful to my biological family and to my Strake Jesuit family."

Br. Gebhard R. M. Fröhlich, SJ
1921 – 2015

Gebhard R.M. Fröhlich was born in lower Silesia (then part of Germany, now Głogów, Poland) on July 2, 1921. Geb attended the equivalent of grade school and high school in Wilthen, Bautzen, and Dresden, Germany. He spent a year as apprentice in pharmacy and two years training in mechanics in Berlin. He had begun a course at Gauss Engineering School in Berlin when he was drafted into the German army in 1941.

From 1941-45 Gebhard served on the Russian Front, constructing railroad installations and bridges during the German advance, and then destroying the same when the Germans retreated before the Russian counter-offensive. He recounts this in a memoir that he wrote many years later, *1944 Etc.: My Many Guardian Angels*. Emerging from the chaos, "I had this deep feeling that God had a plan for me and he was going to make sure that I fulfilled his plan."

Back in Berlin, he began academic art studies in graphics at the Meisterschule für das Kunsthandwerk, where he studied for two years. He also worked at an American officers' club where he made contacts that aided his getting a recommendation allowing him to come to the U.S. He immigrated to the United States in 1949. From 1949-64, he lived and worked mainly in the Miami area doing decorative lighting and setting department store window displays. He first encountered the Society through a Jesuit in Miami. "I did not want to be a priest. The opportunity of being a brother allowed me flexibility in my service of God. The Jesuits offered the intellectually stimulating life I sought."

He began postulancy at Spring Hill College in Mobilem Ala on March 15, 1964, and then started his Novitiate in Grand Coteau, La on September 16, 1964. He pronounced his first vows on September 26, 1966 and later made his Tertianship in Rome, professing his final vows on May 12, 1983.

He studied sculpture at the Academy for Fine Arts and the Academy for Applied Arts in Vienna from 1967-72. With diploma in hand, Geb began his long teaching career in Loyola University's Department of Fine Arts, of which he became Chairman (1974-79). During his time at Loyola, he led several student tours to Europe that focused on art and art history. Beginning in 1991, he became part-time at Loyola when he was made Emeritus Professor. At this

point, he was summoned to Rome to help prepare a special edition of the Society's Yearbook for the Ignatian Year 1991. With failing eyesight, he was finally sent in January 2014 to the St. Alphonsus Rodriguez Pavilion in Grand Coteau. Upon retirement from Loyola, his artistic focus had turned to iconography, including the striking icon of St. Catherine of Siena that stands in the church of that name in New Orleans. He once called the icon, "the perfect spiritual experience: timeless, valuable while at the same time priceless." As his vision deteriorated due to macular degeneration, he observed, "You don't look at an icon. The icon looks at you."

Br. Gebhard R.M. Fröhlich, SJ died in his sleep on January 17, 2015 at the St. Alphonsus Rodriguez Pavilion in Grand Coteau. He was 93 years old and a Jesuit Brother for 50 years. According to his wishes, his body was donated to science.

Br. Joseph P. Gavan, SJ
1910 – 1980

Joseph P. Gavan was born on July 7, 1910. He entered the Order at Grand Coteau, La on October 18, 1931, and after vows he remained at the novitiate for one year as infirmarian, assistant refectorian and "handy man" for the community. He was sent to Spring Hill College in Mobile, Ala for five years (1935-38) as porter and house utility man. It was during this stretch that Joe became an apprentice infirmarian, receiving professional instructions. He returned to Grand Coteau for four years (1940-43) as infirmarian, dispenser of common toiletries and utility Brother. Joe went East again, this time to the House of Studies in Mobile for four years (1944-47), but continuing as infirmarian, dispenser and utility man. In 1947 he added to his labors that of sacristan of the Jesuit church, St. Joseph. Because he had not yet been posted there, Joe was sent to Jesuit High New Orleans for three years (1948-50), where he was oddly not infirmarian, but manager of the community's clothing, assistant porter and, of course, handy man. After one year at St. Joseph's Church (1951), he moved to the tertianship at Pass Christian, Ms for three years (1952-54). After a single year back at Spring Hill College (1955), he returned to Pass Christian for two years as sacristan, infirmarian, manager of the community's clothing and utility brother. Joe became used to orbiting back through Spring Hill, for he immediately spent three years there (1958-60), as infirmarian, clothing manager and domestic postman. In 1962 he began a five-year stint as infirmarian at the Jesuit Stuart Convalescent Home in south Florida (1962-66). And he kept doing his other ministries such sacristan and mailman. Then he traveled to Jesuit High in Tampa where he served for the rest of his Jesuit life (1967-80). He was primarily the school's sacristan, postman, and receptionist. Many Jesuits offered anecdotes and comments about Joe, such as, his rapport with the young students, how likeable he was, and how much Joe himself loved ice cream. On February 28, 1980, Br. Joseph P. Gavan, SJ died; he was sixty-nine years old and forty-nine a Jesuit Brother. John Armstrong, SJ preached the homily at Joe's funeral, from which we take these words:

> [concerning Joe and Ignatian Spiritual Conversation] What Ignatius had in mind was that ability to talk to each person in a way that made the person comfortable – so that the person realized that you thought he was important. By making the person realize this, you are preparing that person for the realization that God also loves him. … When

you spoke to Joe, you always had the feeling that he appreciated your giving a little of your precious time to talk to him. You never felt like he was giving you a little gift of his time on the way to do something more important. That's an art, and a gift. … There was also in Joe certain toughness that one would hardly expect from his fragile exterior. Joe had a tremendously strong sense of duty, and there wasn't much that could stop him from doing what he thought he ought to do. … My pleas with him to let me know when he wasn't feeling well met with an invariable response: "You have enough to worry about."…His rector returned home one night to find a note on his door from Joe: "I have had a small stroke. Nothing to worry about. Could you please come to my room?"

Br. Walter Gonzalez, SJ
1909 – 1981

Walter was born in Mobile, Ala on February 14, 1909. He was educated in the local public schools, after which he worked at various jobs as a manual laborer. He entered the Order at Grand Coteau, La on July 30, 1932 just as the Great Recession grew grim. He remained at the College from 1932 until 1945, working as baker and cook, as well as chauffeur for the community. Obviously he kept his bags packed for he moved across the South from Jesuit institution to Jesuit residence. His first stop on the way was Jesuit High New Orleans, where he worked in the kitchen for three years (1946-49). Then this Mobilian returned to Mobile, that is, to Spring Hill College (1949-57). He spent a year in Augusta, Ga and a year at Manresa Retreat House in Convent, La, after which he worked at the high school in Dallas (1959-62). 1962 was a busy year for him as he went to the high school in New Orleans, but quickly moved to the House of Studies on the Loyola campus, then to the downtown church, and then to Conyers, Ga and wound up in the Provincial residence in Ponchatoula, La (1962-63). He went East to Jesuit High in Tampa, Fla (1963-65), then West to the new Jesuit school in El Paso, Texas (1965-67), then back East to the House of Studies in Mobile (1967-70). He spent a year at Battles Wharf, Ala caring for Fr. Edward Bergan, SJ (1971-72). Then he was back on the road: first at Tampa (1972), then Ponchatoula (1973), the provincial's residence in New Orleans (1974) and then Grand Coteau (1974-75). He was then posted to Montserrat Retreat House in Lake Dallas, Texas in 1975 where he developed a small hermitage. Apparently his baking skills were resurrected, and he treated the staff and the poor people in a neighboring trailer park to his breads. The most common remark made at knowledge of his death was how solicitous he was for people. On January 11, 1981 Br. Walter Gonzalez, SJ died; he was seventy-one years old and forty-nine years as a Jesuit Brother.

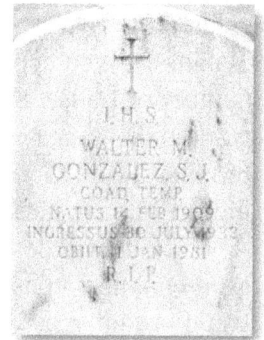

Br. James Walter Gravois, SJ
1930 – 1996

Jimmy was born in Edgard, La on February 10, 1930, the eighth child and the fifth boy. He was educated locally in Edgard, graduating in 1950. After a few months, he entered the Novitiate in Grand Coteau, La on February 16, 1951. And until ill health forced him to move to Ignatius Residence in 1981, he labored for thirty years on the farm which supported the House of Formation. All who labored

with him in the corn fields, the sweet potato patches, etc. marveled at his stamina and good humor. Jimmy was always a giant Jesuit Brother, but one time he went to Weight Watchers and carefully shed over 125 pounds. But the reverse occurred and he regained his former stature. Alas, with fewer tasks to do on the farm, he slowed down his pace, but not his appetite. In time he developed diabetes which grew so severe that he lost one leg. Br. James Walter Gravois, SJ died on August 26, 1996, sixty-six years old and forty-five years a Jesuit Brother.

Br. Alexander Gussio, SJ
1939 – 2017

Alexander Gussio, hereafter called "Gus," was born in Chicago on Valentine's Day, 1939. After his family migrated to Dallas, he attended John Henry Brown elementary school and two years of junior high at Belle Station. Gus entered the Society from there on July 18, 1961. He was encourage by Bob Tynan, SJ, who apparently promised Gus that the Society would teach him a number of trades. Several years later, it was apparent that Gus was unable to work in the trades which were the hallmark of other brothers, skills which was promised him. Gus's superiors verified with Bob Tynan that a promise was indeed made to Gus.

Gus was posted to Our Lady of Guadalupe Parish in San Antonio, Texas, an unknown position which caused Gus anxiety, but after a few weeks he could not imagine being anywhere but San Antonio. On his own he started taking classes in various trades, and became proficient in carpentry, electricity, air conditioning, automobile maintenance and plumbing. Gus' slowness was caused by an illness early in his life. Those who lived with him praised the practical wisdom of being able to read the instructions on how to put something together or how to get some piece of machinery to operate. Before quartz watches, Gus was an able watch repairer; and he is acclaimed as a good barber. Gus had two jobs: not in San Antonio and in San Antonio. He spent two years on the Brothers' Work Crew (1966-68) and then from 1968 until a few months before his death, Guadalupe Church in San Antonio.

Gus had two hobbies. First, model trains for which he had established an imaginative layout. And, second only to the golden lady on the dome, Gus was utterly dedicated to Notre Dame sports.

Gus's hands were good for more than tools. He had come to know many men of trade and some wealthy ones. Though shy and uncomfortable in a group of more than ten people, he was front and center when he saw an opportunity to ask someone for a dollar donation to Guadalupe Church. Gus had a list of people from whom he would ask a donation each month, with the result that at times he could hand the pastor $1,000 and not infrequently more than $1,500. On occasion, he handed over $5000. If we presume that Gus brought in $1500 a month for 540 months, you do the math. In addition, Gus brought in food, especially Polish sausage; he begged bingo gifts from Guadalupe Lumber. And he was the ideal agent to help church groups by selling thousands of their raffle tickets.

This sometime shy Brother came to know and love and assist Jesuit Volunteers in San Antonio since 1985. As he got closer to them, he fed them with pizzas and took them on tours of the Texas Hill Country. More than anyone else at Guadalupe, Gus kept up with a considerable number of the former Jesuit Volunteers. He gavs love and received lots of it in return.

Gus was an attentive and practical person: he kept an eye on the community's cars, reminding the staff to change the oil and get a new license. A bashful beggar? He still invited his benefactors to cross his palm with green support for the church. As Gus said, "Because my friends wear blue collars, sometimes they tell me blues stories, sad stories, painful stories."

Right after Christmas 2016, Gus's health was such that he took up residence in the St. Alphonsus Pavilion at Grand Coteau, La. Six weeks later on February 22, 2017, he died of a massive heart attack. Brother Alex Gussio, SJ was seventy-eight years old when he died, and fifty-six years a Jesuit. Brother.

Br. David J. Henderson, SJ
1882 -1959

David Henderson was born in Glasgow, Scotland on All Saints Day 1882. He was forty-three years old when he entered the Novitiate in Grand Coteau, La on April 18, 1925. Apparently he had considerable experience in construction, for he spent two years more in Grand Coteau as carpenter and ironworker (1927-29), before he transferred to Spring Hill College in Mobile, Ala to do the same tasks there for twelve years (1929-41). Traveling to New Orleans, he took his trade first to Loyola University (1941-44) and then to Jesuit High School (1944-47). When he arrived at the Jesuit church in Shreveport, La, he was no longer assigned to the heavy labor of construction, but to tasks needing lesser stamina, such as receptionist and sacristan (1951-55). Finally he returned to Grand Coteau in retirement to "pray for the Society" for a period of three years. On October 4, 1959, Br. David J. Henderson, SJ died at the age of seventy-six years old and thirty-four as a Jesuit Brother.

Br. Herbert Francis Hinze, SJ
1908 – 2004

Francis Hinze was born in the Methodist environs of Waco, Texas, to be precise, Cego. As we fast forward, we learn that "Frank" read the story of two Jesuits, Martial Lapeyre and George Feltes, who in 1932 landed their crippled aircraft on an ice-covered mountain in Alaska and survived six days in minus 40-degree weather. He was mightily impressed, not only with the event, but that both were Jesuit Brothers. Frank subsequently joined the Catholic church in 1932 and after another year, he entered the Novitiate on April 17, 1933.

Where did this talented man acquire his skills? In 1924 he took a course in architectural drawing. His trademark as a Jesuit Brother was designing buildings and other related projects. A fellow Jesuit once remarked, "Hardly a stick of wood was left over when the building was finished." Frank subsequently organized and planned the construction of two buildings at Loyola University in New Orleans and seven at Spring Hill College in Mobile, Ala. He not only constructed buildings, but equally as important, he was dedicated to their maintenance. Indeed, he headed the maintenance department at Spring Hill College for almost 25 years.

Who was Frank Hinze? He showed great courage in his environment to become a Catholic and a Jesuit Brother. Let us add "fidelity," as evidenced by the many years of steady service. One person said of Frank:"Mild-mannered and always pleasant to deal with, Francis was an expert supervisor of construction and maintenance." As talented as he was in building and maintenance, he also asked to labor in areas unrelated to his field: sacristan, infirmarian, and supervisor of food services. At age 84, Frank was still at work as minister and treasurer of Ignatius Residence, the retirement home in New Orleans.. His decline was occasioned by a serious fall which injured his back. This was followed by a series of strokes that caused him to retreat ever so gently into deeper silence. The substance of Br. Herbert Francis Hinze may be summed up in the Jesuit saying, "The manner was ordinary." But not the depth of his commitment and service. Br. Herbert Francis Hinze, SJ died on February 17, 2004 at the age of ninety-five and seventy-one years a Jesuit Brother.

Br. Robert Earl Hollingsworth, SJ
1930 – 2005

Bob Hollingsworth was born on January 27, 1930 in Linton, Ind. A Baptist by birth, he became a Catholic in 1948. After working a year for Coyne Electric in Chicago, Bob served in a U.S. army tank division in the Korean War (1951-53). He subsequently formed a construction company in Corpus Christi, Texas which specialized in concrete. During a job at Corpus Christi Minor Seminary, he met Tom "Dutch" Jenniskens, SJ, whose Mass he served daily. Bob and Dutch had frequent spiritual conversations, with the result that on February 9, 1962, Bob entered the Novitiate at Grand Coteau, La. He was thirty-four years of age when he pronounced his vows as a Jesuit Brother (1964).

In 1966 Bob joined the New Orleans province mission in Brazil, where he gave almost forty years of devoted service. Besides acting as director and treasurer of the Centro Social Presidente Kennedy in Campinas, he wore many other hats. Ever the constructor, he built *Nossa Senhora de Pompeia* Church, then *Bom Pastor* Church – surely with expert concrete work. Many said that his most important construction project was forming the lives of those in vocational training at Centro Kennedy. In an interview with C. J. McNaspy, SJ, Bob spoke about the *Centro* and what it does. He said:

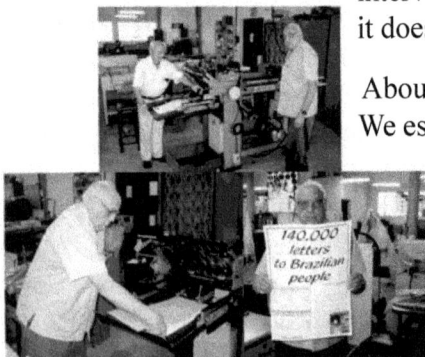

About 1,900 people come here every day for some kind of service. We estimate 456,000 persons per year. … We take care of many of them almost from birth to the grave. Seriously we offer all kinds of services. … We're helping all the immigrants who come to the big city with no preparation. A corporal work of mercy.

Alas, Bob failed to learn Portuguese, yet his colleagues maintain that he truly communicated. When listeners "would turn on their imaginations," they could figure out what he was trying to say. He spoke, they say, the "language of love," and his sense of humor was loud and clear. The best way to measure the success of Bob's labors is to imagine the hundreds of thousands of students who studied at *Centro Kennedy* who were trained there and who now have successful professions, especially in the hospitals of the region.

Bob was a pious and dedicated leader – remember that he was an officer in an Army tank division. He exuded competence and so confidence. One boy said of Bob, "He was always positive and never complained." A girl said that he was never able to pronounce her name, Zoraide," so Bob called her Dona. Bob was, she said, "her friend." Where, now, is the formidable man who entered the Novitiate in 1962? Some described him as "the suffering servant who did not open his mouth." He began to have health problems, but leaving Brazil was not an option. On September 25, 2005, Br. Robert Earl Hollingsworth. SJ died in Campinas, São Paulo, Brazil at the age of seventy-five and forty-three years a Jesuit Brother.

Br. Lawrence J. Huck, SJ
1969 – 20??

The twins, Larry and Lloyd Huck, were born on February 7, 1969. Eventually the family expanded with the births of Mary, Jimmy, Kerry, Johnny and Lynette. After graduating from Jesuit High New Orleans, he proved that he could do two things at the same time: attend the University of New Orleans and work in his father's electrical business. While he earned no college degree then, he was awarded in 1990 the status of Master Electrician. A vocation was blowing in the wind for a long time, "… after all, I was raised in a good Catholic family." Larry was already apprenticing as a "man for others," with service in the cerebral palsy camp and assisting in the CYO. A significant moment came with Lloyd's marriage. Now Larry thought seriously "I need something to do. … What do you want to do that will make you happy?" Larry then applied to the Society and entered the Novitiate at Grand Coteau, La on Aug 14, 1993 as a Brother. Here he experienced more and intenser confirmation. After vows he was sent to Creighton University for three years, focusing on the humanities, ending up with a BA in History (1995-98). This confirmed that Larry could handle intellectual things, as well as electricity.

He served for four years during his Regency in Tampa, Fla from 1998 until 2002, teaching History, serving in campus ministry and as director of community service. Larry then matriculated for three years (2002-04) at the Jesuit School of Theology in Berkeley, Calif, finishing with a MTS in Spirituality. Thus equipped, he went to Jesuit High in New Orleans to teach for five years (2004-09); he taught courses on the Sacraments, and eventually took over the Seniors' prayer class. Finally, he made his tertianship in Dublin, Ireland (2009-10) and pronounced his final vows on July 29, 2012.

All of the above, while accurate, does not describe Larry Huck. Because he is a handsome, intelligent extrovert who is a Jesuit Brother, he became the poster child for the vocation of Jesuit Brothers. He arranged for an assistancy-wide meeting of Brothers at Creighton in 1999: "Jesuits in the Millennium." He organized and hosted a conference called "Jesuits in the New Media" (2013).

Talk about "giving back!" Larry was appointed to supervise the two-year, multi-million-dollar renovation of St. Charles College in Grand Coteau. He served as the owner's agent in the process. He was splendidly prepared for the extensive metamorphosis of the hundred-year old facility into a modern structure where plumbing, electricity and a hundred more things were brought up to code. Of course, he found time to teach physics to the boys at St. John Berchmans' Academy, the new addition to the Academy of the Sacred Heart.

As evidence of his standing in the province, he was named a consultor of the province for six years, and for the newly combined Central and Southern Province for two more years. He was appointed as the first full-time president of Good Shepherd School in New Orleans. He describes his relationship with the faculty as having *cura personalis* of the people under him. He loves to be with people and is dedicated to the school.

Br. Michael Kiernan, SJ
1895 – 1939

Michael Kiernan, a native of Alabama, was born on July 11, 1895 and entered the Novitiate in Macon, Ga on May 15, 1920. He was posted to Grand Coteau, La for the next sixteen years (1922-38). He served in many capacities: supervisor of the kitchen, infirmarian, assistant tailor, dispenser of the common supplies, czar of the chickens, director of novices' chores, and farmer par excellence. Br. Michael Kiernan, SJ died on March 13, 1939. He was nineteen years a Jesuit Brother and only forty-four years old.

Br. Gerald Joseph Landry, SJ
1933 – 2014

Gerry and his twin brother were born in Jeanerette, La on November 9, 1933, and were educated locally. After graduation in 1952, he enlisted in the US Air Force for a period of four years. After this Gerry tried the seminary and then spent several years at USL (now grown into the University of Louisiana at Lafayette). His attraction to the Jesuits climaxed when on October 20, 1959 Gerry began his postulancy at Spring Hill College in Mobile, Ala to become a Jesuit Brother. He pronounced his first vows on April 27, 1962. Like most Brothers at that time, he did not go to college for a specific training.

Yet Gerry might be said to have interned to be an infirmarian. His first ten years as a Jesuit Brother were focused exclusively on this job. He spent six years at St. Charles College in Grand Coteau, La in this work (1959-65). When posted to Spring Hill College, he served as infirmarian for one year (1965-66) and then moved to the Jesuit House of Studies for three years in the same capacity (1966-69). As he made his tour of the province, Gerry was assigned to a new post, minister of the community at Loyola University New Orleans (1969-74). He returned to Spring Hill College as the Director of Student Activities, a position he held for eleven years (1974-85).

This was his only major assignment where he worked with people other than Jesuits. But it was as an efficient Brother minister that he completed his labors. He spent eleven years at Strake Jesuit College Prepratory in Houston, Texas as its minister (1986-97), and then from 1997 until 2014 he served at Jesuit High in Dallas, Texas as the community's minister and business office assistant. Br. Gerald Joseph Landry, SJ died on December 6, 2014 at Grand Coteau, two days after he joined the Pavilion of St. Alphonsus Rodriguez. He was 81 years old, and a Jesuit Brother for 55 years.

On the occasion of his Jubilee (2003), Gerry wrote:

> Community life has always been a very great attraction for me, and perhaps that is why I chose the Society of Jesus. ... I am grateful for a special person who has helped me during trials in the early stages of life in the Society. I have learned many things in the Jesuits, but the one that sticks out the most is learning to be patient with others and being attentive to their needs.

Br. Martial Octave Lapeyre, SJ
1908 – 1989

Martial was born on September16, 1908 in New Orleans into a socially prominent family. Four children followed religious vocations, two into the sisterhood, one as a Jesuit priest and one as a Jesuit brother. Shortly after he graduated from Jesuit High New Orleans, he entered the Novitiate at Grand Coteau, La on August 14, 1926. From 1927 to 1963 he plied his considerable talent in the field of mechanics, even two years in aviation in Alaska. Martial might well have embroidered on his shirts: "Mechanic: if it's metal and it moves, it is mine." Because he was so useful to pastoral and academic communities, he was always on the move, basically oscillating between Spring Hill College in Mobile, Ala and Grand Coteau. Yes, he was a master of making machines work (esp. canning machines), but he possessed other valuable skills, such as carpentry and remodeling of rooms, which his superiors ordered him to use. But his talent and personality were channeled into a special project, the Brothers' Training Program, which taught Brothers how to learn new skills and attain competency in them. Most definitely Martial was a key figure in shaping the education and capabilities of the Brothers of the twentieth century. In 1957 he was made the press manager of the Jesuit publication Revista Catolica at El Paso, Texas, which closed in 1963. Perhaps his hard labors were over, but he remained a whizz at institutional maintenance; and his organizational skills identified him as a good house minister. He alternated these skills in his eighty-one years at the new Jesuit College Prep in Dallas (1977-1989) and at Montserrat Retreat House in Lake Dallas (1973-77).

Martial is immortalized in the lore of the province for his plane crash on an icy mountain in Alaska. Early in his Jesuit life he conceived of a desire to go on the Alaska mission as a pilot. Thus he took a correspondence course in flying and started taking flying lessons. In 1931 he went to New York to pick up a plane paid for in part by one of his sisters. Once in Alaska he and Brother George Feltes had to make a crash landing on a mountain. Because of bad weather they endured six days of -40 weather with very little fuel or food. They were rescued; his superior sold the plane and Martial returned to Grand Coteau (1931-33).

Later in time, Br. Feltes said of Martial: "Over the years, Brother Lapeyre made a great reputation as a holy and talented brother." Tom Clancy, SJ repeated the same thing in his profile of Martial in *Friends*, 1st Edition: "In his lifetime there was probably no other Jesuit in the province more in demand then 'Lap.' It was easy to see why. He was a hard worker who could fix anything. He lived poorly, never complained, and got along with everyone. He had a shy self-deprecating sense of humor and great patience with those less blessed with talent and energy." Br. Martial Lapeyre, SJ, worn out with good works, died on April 18, 1989. He was eighty years old and sixty-three years a Jesuit Brother.

Br. Roy Charles Lavergne, SJ
1918 – 1967

Roy Charles Lavergne was born in Louisiana's Acadia Parish on July 28, 1918. He worked on the family farm for a number of years and then labored as a service station operator. In August of 1945 he applied for entrance into the Order, but was refused because of a heart condition. A decade later, he was directed to Dr. Michael De Bakey, a premier heart surgeon in Houston, who performed a successful operation. Two years later in 1957 Roy knocked on the Novitiate door once more. Without the heart condition he was readily accepted as a Jesuit Brother novice. His signature craft in the Society was that of tailor: he sewed two and even three cassocks a day. And he acted as receptionist, a natural fit because of his relaxed voice. Roy was a Jesuit of great modesty; he was truly "indifferent" to whatever God wished and he was a steady, spiritual man. He was what is called a "regular" man. The old ways were good, and the new Vatican II ways were mysterious and abrasive to him. On January 6, 1967 Br. Roy Charles Lavergne, SJ suffered a fatal heart attack and no amount of assistance could rescue him. He was forty-eight years old and ten years a Jesuit Brother.

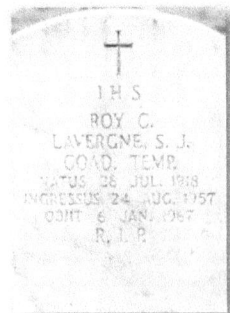

Br. Dennis Lonergan, SJ
1928 – 2002

Dennis Patrick Lonergan was born in New Orleans on April 7, 1928 into a family of six siblings. After primary schooling at St. Rita's, he attended Jesuit High, from which he graduated in 1945. He began his postulancy immediately, and after six months, on March 16, 1946, he entered the Novitiate. He remained at Grand Coteau, La for five years after vows, becoming acquainted with the crafts that would become his signature contributions to the province: baker and assistant cook, buyer, and carpenter (1948-52). While at Grand Coteau, he had the benefit of being mentored by some of the province's great Jesuit Brothers: Martial Lapeyre, Frank Hinze, and Michael Moore. He was next posted to Assumption Hall at Spring Hill College in Mobile, Ala from 1953 to 1956, in the area of food production and food service: refectorian, king of the kitchen, buyer and the person in charge of renovation and repair. He would become famous in the province for his culinary skill, for he loved to cook what everyone loved to eat. He spent two years at the Immaculate Conception Church in New Orleans as sacristan (1957-58). After tertianship in El Paso, Texas, he remained there at the new high school as carpenter and electrician, prefect of discipline in the students' dining hall, mechanic for the Jesuits' cars and moderator of the photography club (1959-62). At Jesuit High in New Orleans, he was refectorian, as well as occasional receptionist and keeper of the clothes closet (1963-67). He was then assigned to the Jesuit Institutional Maintenance Corps, a team of Jesuit Brothers who traveled from community to community doing renovation and repair (1968-71).

His ministry took a sharp turn when he was appointed Brother minister of the provincial's residence in New Orleans (1972-75). The province built on this success and assigned him to Loyola University in the same capacity (1976-78); his advice was judged worthy and so he was appointed a consultor for the community. He returned to the provincial's residence as Brother Minister, a position he held from 1978 to 1990. When the retirement home, Ignatius Residence, moved to the building of the former provincial's dwelling, he became the custodian of its grounds and of the kitchen; again he was asked his advice on local matters for he was made a house consultor (1991-2000). In time he was not simply working at Ignatius Residence, but a member of its retirement community. He was famous in the province for his zeal for the local football team, the Saints, and also for the vesuvial explosions at their failures. On May 22, 2002, Br. Dennis Lonergan, SJ died. He was seventy-four years old and fifty-seven years a Jesuit Brother. These remarks come from an obituary written by a Jesuit who lived with Dennis and knew him well:

> Dennis was a pleasant companion; I lived with him for about 7 years. He loved villa, became a good water skier and loved to fish. I mention his attraction to the Charismatics. But Dennis always showed a deep sense of spirituality. And I believe, lived his Jesuit life very well. He had a good sense of humor and play. Yes, he had a quick temper, but it never lasted, and, as Pope Francis says, who am I to throw the first stone (May 3, 2014).

Br. Lawrence J. Lundin, SJ
1947 – 20??

Larry Lundin is one of the dozens of candidates to the Society who came from Dallas, Texas in the 1960s and 70s. Larry, born on Oct 15, 1947, the last of four children of Charles Bernard and May Belle Pecot Lundin. Larry was educated at Christ the King Church (1953-62) and then at Jesuit High of Dallas (1962-66). His association with the Order deepened as Larry fulfilled his work-grant by answering phones both days and weekends at the school. He entered the Novitiate at Grand Coteau , La on Jan 15, 1967. He says that he was particularly enriched by contact with Brothers Mock and Usina at Jesuit, and then in the Novitiate with association with the province's quartet of outstanding Brothers: Lloyd Barry, Michael Moore, Hilliard Stiegler, and Martial Lapeyre. While a junior Brother, he pursued a degree in accounting at the University of Southwest Louisiana, graduating with a BA in 1971. As he earned his bachelor's degree, he assisted Br. Hillard Stiegler in the Grand Coteau treasurer's office. With this skill set, he was assigned as assistant treasurer of the province then located

in New Orleans, and with this professional practice under his belt, he pursued an MBA at Loyola New Orleans (1976), laboring day and night.

His next assignment took him to Wheeling Jesuit University in West Virginia for one year and then to the heart of the province, St. Charles College in Grand Coteau, as minister, treasurer and kitchen manager (1976-80), then off to the East to Jesuit High in Tampa, Fla as minister, athletic business manager, teacher and guest master (1980-84), then North to the Jesuit Conference in Washington, DC as Secretary for Finance (1984-89), and then to a sabbatical at the Franciscan Center in Santa Barbara, Calif (1989-90).

Finally Larry returned to the Jesuit Provincial Office in New Orleans as its treasurer. His dossier says that he held this job for twenty-two years (1990-2012). How easy to print the dates, but how hard to imagine all that the job entailed. He kept up the flow of funds for communities in the province and for its members living and working elsewhere. Twenty-two years! Yet, as Larry himself said, "In all these places the work was great and there was good support from the Jesuit Communities, friends and work colleagues." During this time he went to Cuernavaca to learn Spanish (1990).

Father Provincial asked Larry to work on the project undertaken by sixteen religious institutes in New Orleans to build Our Lady of Wisdom Healthcare Center, a task he completed in association with Sister Majorie Hebert, MSC, adding as well his services as its treasurer and board member for about 14 years. Of course, he continued his assigned duties at the provincial's office. After twenty-two years as province treasurer, he enjoyed a brief sabbatical. As Missouri and New Orleans began to merge into the Central and Southern Province, Larry served as the New Orleans agent in assisting the formation of a treasurer's job in St. Louis (2012-13).

At the beginning of 2013, Larry moved to Washington to the Gonzaga Jesuit Community and began to work in Silver Springs, Md at the Resource Center for Religious Institutes, where he serves as Assistant Director of Administration and Finance. Although Larry could never be said to seek approval or recognition, others showed him the respect he deserved. He was selected as one of three brothers to receive national recognition, the "2003 Annual Brotherhood Award." The citation for Larry Lundin reads:

> He has shared his time, talents, and many skills in the area of Finance and Accounting while at the same time showing a compassionate presence and concern for the elderly religious of his community. His years as Province treasurer have earned him the respect of bankers and financiers who have been instrumental in offering sound advice to the Province. A man of prayer, Brother has exhibited special qualities of humility, trustworthiness, integrity, work ethics, a sense of humor and commitment to Religious Life.

In addition, he received the Trustee of the Year award from the Leading Age Gulf Coast Association of Homes and Services to the Aged (2012). The only thing that remains is God's ultimate Seal of Approval.

Br. George Magrath, SJ
1882 – 1945

Although George Magrath was born in Brooklyn, NY on November 10, 1882, we are sure that he did not come South as a carpetbagger. He entered the Novitiate at Macon, Ga on July 20, 1901, just shy of being nineteen years old. His first assignment was to Spring Hill College in Mobile, Ala to begin learning a series of tasks which did not require stamina or skill: refectorian, dispenser of the common closet, and finally house manager. For sixteen years George served both in the Jesuit quarters and also in the college (1903-19). He seems to have enjoyed long tenure in the houses where he worked, and then he went to Shreveport, La to labor for fifteen years (1919-34). While there he continued with the jobs he had previously done, adding to them receptionist and sacristan. He made a brief three-year stop at Loyola University in New Orleans as it refectorian and table reader (1934-37). Then it was back to Shreveport for eight more years, six years at the high school and two years at the parish. Br. George Magrath, SJ died in Shreveport on November 8, 1945; he was sixty-three years old and thirty-two as a Jesuit Brother.

Br. James J. Maitland, SJ
1907 – 1976

James Joseph Maitland was born in Belize, British Honduras on May 24, 1907. The only thing we know about his education is that he was an alumnus of Loyola University, New Orleans, for him a most auspicious beginning. He entered the Order on December 23, 1934. His first assignment was as sacristan of Holy Name of Jesus, New Orleans for four years (1938-42). While there, he was moderator of the Altar Boys and the CYO, early evidence of how well he would get along with people. After Tertianship and final vows, Jimmy returned to New Orleans, specifically to Loyola University where he served for the rest of his life. His assignment in the community included "Assistant Procurator of the Jesuit Community (1945-1968), along with Director of the kitchen (1947-51), sacristan for the Jesuit house (1955-67) and Procurator of the community (1969-76). What kind of man was he? The Province obit stated: "'He was one hell-of-a-good fellow,' was one of Brother James J. Maitland's exuberant ways of recalling just about anyone he knew. Jimmy was a fine judge of human nature. But he was still more charitable. The description applies most of all to himself."

We are fortunate to have an editorial about Jimmy written and delivered on WWL-TV by Phil Johnson:

The news story was brief and to the point. A man named James Maitland had died at age 69. He was a Jesuit Brother for 42 years, at Loyola for 38 years. Mourned by all. End of story. But not really. James Maitland, or Brother Jimmy, as he was known to everyone, was a quiet little man, but a man, whose introspection masked a great earthy wisdom, whose humility covered a masterful sense of humanity. He was a simple man, with simple tastes. And yet he had the magical faculty of penetrating subterfuge and facade. He was not fooled by many people. He suffered the foolish. He spotted the phonies. He was a good friend of candor and genuineness. He had three great passions in life, fishing, photography, and the New York Yankees. And he pursued all with the eagerness and vigor of a youth. He was just a quiet little man. Yet now that he's gone we realize that his life touched many people. And all are better, somehow, for having known him. Because of Brother Jimmy having been here, the world is a better place. That's quite an epitaph for any man.

Brother James Joseph Maitland, SJ suffered a heart attack in 1974, and was felled by a second attack in 1976. He was 69 years old and a Jesuit Brother for 42 years. This "little man" was a large oak in the Order.

Br. Alcide Joseph Martin, SJ
1929 – 2017

Most people think of Plaquemine, La as Joe's home town, but he was born on June 25, 1929 in Maringouin and christened in Grosse Tête. After high school, Joe attended LSU for three years (1945-48), earning a B.B.S. degree. With the Korean war escalating, Joe served in the Army Signal Corps for several years (1951-53). The following year, Joe entered the Novitiate on March 15, 1954.

Joe manifested considerable organizational ability, especially in regard to the most sensitive area in the life of a community: food and service. His career as a Jesuit Brother was born in the kitchen of Grand Coteau, La (1960-66), the quality of whose meals we could know only when we moved on. Once Brothers could become ministers of the community, Joe served in that administrative capacity for forty-five years: at Jesuit High New Orleans (1966-73), Strake Jesuit College Preparatory in Houston, Texas (1973-79), Ignatius Residence in New Orleans (1979-81), again Jesuit New Orleans (1981-84), Loyola University (1985-92), and Jesuit High in Tampa, Fla (1992-2003). Finally, Joe wound up where he had begun, as kitchen manager of St. Charles College (2003-10). But a good minister was more than a kitchen czar; and to him was entrusted the maintenance of the house and its autos. He might also be the superintendent of buildings and grounds, when called upon.

Joe's talent extended into ministries having to do with accounting and finance. Management by a Brother Minister involved finances, of which Joe acquitted himself well. Moreover, he worked on the staff of the Jesuit Seminary and Mission Bureau (1981-84), even as he served as minister and treasurer to several Jesuit communities in New Orleans.

Joe was the kind of minister who understood that his job was to make resources available, and not to restrict their flow. It did not take much investigation to learn how important to him was his service of his community. Certainly no one would accuse Joe of being a miser. And he had good judgment about what facilities or furnishings were needed for a community. While many have been blistered by Joe's eruptions, he was always a good companion.

It came to light that Joe had serious heart disease. In addition to coronary arrest in Tampa, Joe eventually had four heart valve replacements. The return to Grand Coteau was intended to lighten his labors. He was the kitchen manager there until he needed assisted living care and so moved to St. Alphonsus Rodriguez Pavilion in July of 2013. He died there just as this book was going to press on December 4, 2017.

Br. Edward McCarten, SJ
1872 – 1949

Edward McCarten was born in Preston, England on June 5, 1872. After emigrating to America, he entered the Novitiate at Macon, Ga on July 25, 1889. In one capacity or another, his entire Jesuit ministry as a Brother was linked with food preparation and presentation. After one year as apprentice cook at Macon, he began to serve as refectorian. After moving to Spring Hill College in Mobile, Ala, Edward spent nine years as refectorian, and was in charge of the community's common supplies (1894-1903). He was next posted to New Orleans, first to the Jesuit residence where he added cooking to his culinary repertoire (1903-04). With the birth of Loyola University, he went uptown to continue as refectorian for nine years, as well as keeper of the common closet, sacristan, lamplighter and receptionist (1904-13). He was next posted to Jesuit High in Tampa, Fla where he continued the same tasks as he had in New Orleans, with the addition of being infirmarian (1913-26). After a three-year stay at Spring Hill College (1926-29), he returned to Tampa to serve for nineteen years; his duties were much reduced now because he was aging (1929-48). He was brought to the province infirmary at Grand Coteau, La in 1948, where his only assignment was to pray for the Society. Br. Edward McCarten, SJ died on March 4, 1949. He was sixty years a Jesuit Brother and seventy-six years old.

Br. John McNulty, SJ
1826 – 1896

John McNulty, the eldest of fourteen children, was born in Roscommon, Ireland on March 25, 1826. He delayed marriage until he had provided security for his thirteen siblings. Then he set out with his young wife for New Orleans, where he soon acquired a prosperous business and a good social standing. But his wife died and he entrusted his son and daughter to the schools of the Jesuits and Sacred Heart Religious in America and Europe. His daughter joined the Religious of the Sacred Heart in Grand Coteau, La and became a very accomplished woman. When his son was settled, John was free at sixty years old to give his life to God in humble service. On October 5, 1886, he entered the Novitiate of St. Stanislaus in Macon, Ga. A fine-featured, educated gentleman, John was at home at once with the Brothers, cheering them by ready wit and story and knowing kindness. As buyer and assistant treasurer he did much to soften anti-Catholic prejudice in Macon. When called to Grand Coteau in 1896, Brother John caught his first disease and died of it on Christmas morning 1896. He was seventy years old and a Jesuit Brother for ten years.

Br. Leo A. McCarty, SJ
1897 – 1942

Leo McCarty, a native Alabamian, was born on August 19, 1897 and entered the Order at the Novitiate at Grand Coteau, La on October 6, 1931. From his very first assignment, it was evident that Leo McCarty was an educated man. In addition to being the manager of the kitchen, he served as associate treasurer and at related jobs such as house buyer and dispenser of common supplies. His talent attracted the eye of Father Provincial who made him his Brother Socius, a job he held for five years (1936-41). Leo returned to the Novitiate where he continued his work as buyer and now as assistant infirmarian. Br. Leo A. McCarty, SJ died on February 4, 1942, young at forty-four years old and eleven as a Jesuit.

Br. Michael Joseph Moore, SJ
1913 – 2000

After graduating from McGill Institute in Mobile, Ala, Michael Joseph Moore attended Spring Hill College briefly. Four years later, he entered the Novitiate on February 2, 1940 as a Brother, several years before his brother, John, entered the Order to be a Priest. "What did Brother Moore do?" He did everything, as well as possible and as frugally as he could. His responsibilities went as low as the college's boiler and as high as its water tower. Whatever the system, Brother Moore kept it working.

His personal papers contain endless lists: Roman emperors, ancient measures and their modern equivalents, the ideal formula for an enema, modern and especially Irish saints, etc. He had lists of the province Brothers: by age, by seniority, and by date of birth. Michael continued to educate himself by working through the progressive stages of serious mathematics. His own brother states that Michael was an autodidact: he taught himself everything he wanted or needed to know.

Michael taught math and technical skills to young Brothers, but not in class. He assigned each an individual project, monitored and corrected it. If there was an error, he never said where it was, but required his student to find it on his own. Br. Terry Todd narrates that when he asked Michael to teach him three-phase electricity, Michael said that he did not know this, which dismayed Br. Todd. But a few days later Michael handed Terry a single sheet of paper with an accurate, precise treatise on three-phase electricity.

Only because of Michael's many lists, do we have a chronological report of his health. He always had many serious aches and pains – of which no one knew. He had the prudence to consult a doctor about the acute arthritic condition of both shoulders and a compressed fracture of his lower spine. Observing him, however, one would never image the pain he lived with.

Michael's life is hard to narrate because he constantly lived an ordinary life in which he was never the center of attention. Simplicity, frugality, and humility best describe Michael. His brother John states that he entered the Jesuits with the same ascetical habits and attitudes characteristic of a mature Jesuit. Yet Michael liked to make funny, so that only those close to him found "a monk who was cheerful, recollected, good humored." When Brother Moore took vows in 1950, the Rector asked him to speak. "I have nothing to say," said he, and sat down. Next year when asked to speak, Michael stood and said, "Last year I had nothing to say; this year the grandeur of the occasion renders me speechless."

Photos of his room testify to the exquisite simplicity of his life: no air conditioning, only a fan (think of Grand Coteau in the summer!), only an essential desk and chair, a rocking chair – foisted upon him – a medicine cabinet – empty; a six-shelved bookcase with only prayer books, *Friends*, and his copy books. No pictures on the walls, no carpet on the floor. His armoire contained only four work shirts, underwear; a coat and shoes (work boots/day shoes). Br. Michael Joseph Moore, SJ was authentic in his Jesuit life – which is why so many admired him and respected him. He died on September 16, 2000; he was eighty-seven years old and a Jesuit Brother for sixty years.

Br. George Anthony Murphy, SJ
1922 – 2011

George Anthony Murphy was born in Macon, Ga on October 11, 1922. His father had emigrated from England to Lowell because he was a skilled textile worker. Soon he was sent to the headquarters of his employer located in Macon. When George was ready for college, he attended Spring Hill College in Mobile, Ala and entered the Novitiate in Grand Coteau, La on August 14, 1941. George was accepted into the track for ordained Jesuit ministry. He was educated in the humanities in the Juniorate and in philosophy at Spring Hill College; he spent his Regency in Shreveport, La; then he studied theology at St. Marys, Kansas for two years. But instead of ordination, George returned to the province to teach for three years. In this time of discernment, George was told that he did not have a priestly vocation, so his superior then asked if he wished to become a Jesuit Brother. He was accepted and made the obligatory second Novitiate.

In 1960 George earned a Certificate in Library Science from Loyola University in New Orleans which determined the direction of his ministry for years to come. When a Jesuit high school was opened in El Paso, Texas, George became its librarian for eleven years (1961-72). When the school closed, he brought its library to the Jesuit school in Houston and served as librarian there. He moved east to Grand Coteau and its library, and then to the Provincial's Residence in New Orleans. Loretto Academy in El Paso needed a librarian, so George returned there to do his signature ministry. While in El Paso he became associated with Fr. Dick Thomas, SJ and his work with the neediest. In 1977 George was missioned to Corpus Christi Minor Seminary, where he served as assistant librarian. George had made a fast friend of Tom Egan, SJ who had been assigned to the Shrine of the North American Martyrs in Auriesville, NY. Since George had no place to stay during the summers, he spent the time with Tom at the Shrine.

In 1982 George was posted to Grand Coteau as librarian, assistant treasurer and guestmaster. Many famous Jesuit Brothers have been porters, receptionists and guestmasters, and George belongs in their company. Often he would fetch retreatants for the Spirituality Center from the airport, bus terminal, and train station in Lafayette; to be sure, he brought them back for departure. Moreover, as guestmaster he greeted arrivals and showed them to their rooms, often detouring to give them a tour of St. Charles College. He was the soul of hospitality, a grace for which many kept in close touch with him later. This glorious harvest lasted twenty-two years.

George was much concerned at the low number of recruits to be Jesuit Brothers. So he persuaded fellow Jesuits and lay associates among the retreatants to pray fervently on the first Monday of the month for vocations. He regularly sent those on his mailing list a reminder and a pious reflection. Threatened with a major illness, George went to Ignatius Residence in New Orleans. Fortunately, he did not need treatment, nevertheless he remained there in a new assignment, to pray for the Church and the Society. Br. George Anthony Murphy, SJ died on Nov 19, 2011. He was eighty-nine years old and seventy years a Jesuit.

Br. Alfred Michael Nowak, SJ
1916 – 1998

Alfred Michael Nowak was born in Buffalo, NY on September 24, 1916 into a family of four children. After his tenth grade, he left school, and immediately entered the Novitiate at Grand Coteau, La on Jan 18, 1935. Inasmuch as he brought no particular skill or trade into the Order, he became a "utility infielder," such as supervisor of the laundry at Grand Coteau (1937-39). After this he acted as the cook, refectorian, maintenance man and sacristan in most of the Jesuit houses from El Paso, Texas to Miami, Fla. He was mostly assigned to the high schools of the province for a total of twenty–five of his years as a Brother. Because of his skill in maintenance, he was tapped for the retreat house in Pass Christian, Miss (1958-59), Spring Hill College in Mobile, Ala (1965-70), Loyola University (1970-76) and the churches in downtown New Orleans (1976-81) and Miami, Fla (1981-94). For almost fifteen years, Al served as the sacristan of the Gesú in Miami; and his judgment was proved valuable when he was made a house consultor. Because of his friendship with cigarettes, he eventually developed lung cancer. Surgery seemed to have removed the malignancy, but several years later it was discovered to have metastasized. In 1995, he moved to Ignatius Residence in New Orleans to "pray for the Church and the Society." Two days before he died, after receiving Viaticum, the community asked him individually for forgiveness for all that they had done to him intentionally or unintentionally. At the end of the ceremony, each one shook hands with him. He saw his life as a difficult one, and he too asked forgiveness for being hard on his brothers. On January 14, 1998, Br. Alfred Michael Nowak, SJ died. He was eighty-one years old and sixty-one years a Jesuit Brother.

Br. Ferdinand Peter, SJ
1863 – 1939

Ferdinand Peter is one of the rare Austrians to become a Jesuit of the New Orleans province. He was born on April 26, 1863 in Tisis, Austria. He entered the Order on April 10, 1884 at Macon, Ga. For every one of the fifty-five years of his Jesuit life, he served as sacristan of the college church in downtown New Orleans. In 1903 he took on the task of herding the students to their worship in the school's church, a task he performed for thirty-six years. Br. Ferdinand Peter, SJ died on July 10, 1939 when he was seventy-six years old and fifty-five as a Jesuit Brother.

Br. James Lee Phillips, SJ
1930 – 1968

"Lee," as he was called, was born in Mobile, Ala on February 5, 1930. After a modest amount of schooling, Lee entered the Novitiate in Grand Coteau, La on August 29, 1948. Subsequently he remained at St. Charles College for six years (1951-56), during which his exclusive task was that of refectorian. He was then sent to the House of Studies in Mobile as refectorian and receptionist, to which was added the task of launderer (1957-59). He went West to the new Jesuit high school in El Paso, Texas, where he continued as refectorian, launderer and now custodian of the wine cellar; his tasks there expanded to include director of the office of information and sacristan (1960-67). He went to the high school in Shreveport, La for only one year as sacristan, shepherd of the altar boys, leader of the local Boy Scouts and the junior CYO. Br. James Lee Phillips, SJ died on July 20, 1968, thirty-eight years old and twenty-years a Jesuit.

In his obituary, Ignatius Fabacher, SJ made several important points about Lee Phillips, well worth repeating:

> His efficiency in material affairs was never an exceptional characteristic with him; but the efficiency with which he endeared himself to his religious brethren was unsurpassed.... His years in El Paso, Texas testify that he labored long into the night for the people he learned to love, no matter whether they were little people or big people, rich people or poor people, lettered or unlettered. He seemed to be doing the Corporal Works of Mercy, of feeding the hungry, giving drink to the thirsty, clothing the naked, harboring the poor, visiting the imprisoned in jail or detention home, visiting the sick or burying the dead..

Br. John Edward Puza, SJ
1933 – 20??

All of his life John Puza has been comically different from his religious brothers. He was born in McAdoo, Penn on January 17, 1933, baptized at St. Kunegunda Church and received his primary education at the school of the same name (1939-46). He graduated from McAdoo High in 1950. John subsequently served in the Army (1953-55). After service John worked to make a living. He is rumored to have been an excellent barber.

And then it happened: John felt called to be a Jesuit Brother, and so on March 3, 1966 he entered the Novitiate in Grand Coteau, La. John had many different assignments and appeared to be a man in serious motion. He was posted to Jesuit High in Tampa, Fla for five years (1968-73), then Spring Hill College in Mobile, Ala (1973-76). His trajectory was like an orbit: Spring Hill, then Jesuit High Shreveport, La (1976-79) and back to Spring Hill College (1979-83). Then John stepped into a new world with an assignment to teach in St. Ignatius grade school in Grand Coteau (1983-85); he would return to this ministry. He became the minister for Strake Jesuit in Houston, Texas for one year (1985-86) and he stayed on as assistant prefect of discipline for another year (1986-87). Then he was cast to the Cubans for four years at Belen Jesuit High School in Miami, Fla (1987-91). He returned to Grand Coteau to teach fourteen more years at St. Ignatius Elementary School (1991-2005). His road then led him to Mobile where he served as an assistant at L'Arche Mobile (2005-2007). He retired and spent time at Our Lady of Wisdom in New Orleans; his only mission now was "to pray for the Church and the Society." Yet he hit the road once more, becoming the assistant to the superior at Jesuit High Tampa (2009-10). Finally he became fully retired at Ignatius Residence in New Orleans and later at the St. Alphonsus Pavilion in Grand Coteau (2013-). John was blessed with a certain irreverence, which honeyed his conversation. As one would expect, he looked critically at any pretense in Jesuits better educated or seated on administrative thrones. As he aged, he qualified as one of the province's eccentrics. Who else would wear cut-offs and style his long white hair in a pony tail and whistle as he went?

Br. Edwin W. Rareshide, SJ
1882 – 1943

Edwin W. Rareshide was born in New Orleans on June 21, 1882. When he was fifty years old, he entered the Society of Jesus on October 13, 1931 at the Novitiate in Grand Coteau, La. After vows, he remained there for one year as apprentice for various jobs: custodian of the clothing closet and infirmarian. He spent one year at Loyola University New Orleans as its infirmarian (1934-35), and then returned to Grand Coteau for the rest of his days. He resumed care for the clothing closet and became the general maintenance man for St. Charles College from 1935 to 1942. For the last two years of his life he resided in the infirmary, suffering from a variety of illnesses. Br. Edwin W. Rareshide, SJ died on February 7, 1943, sixty-one years old and twelve a Jesuit Brother.

Br. James Joseph Remich, SJ
1919 – 2012

After graduation from high school, he worked for five years in the family business and might have continued except for the military draft (1936-41). Inducted into the Army, he served his tour of duty in the South Pacific (1942-45), surviving the battles which brought down the Japanese Empire. After his discharge, he continued to serve Uncle Sam, this time in the US Post Office (1945-59). On January 15, 1960 he entered the Novitiate at Grand Coteau, La and broke the rule by taking four years of college, studying alongside the Scholastics in the Juniorate (1959-63), but there is no note that he earned a college degree. In 1963 Joe moved to the Provincial's Office in New Orleans where he worked from 1963-2003. Joe was clear-minded, steady and not intimidated by finances, so he served the province as treasurer in a variety of ways. Initially he was the assistant treasurer for the province (1963-72); then he was enshrined as the province treasurer, a service he rendered for eighteen solid years (1972-90). After this he became the treasurer of the Jesuit Seminary and Mission Bureau (1990-2001). All the while he also served as the revisor for the province, that is, he was the province accountant who traveled to schools and parishes to examine their books. As time began to catch up with him, he kept his revisor job, but only as an assistant. In 2004 Joe was missioned to Ignatius Residence in New Orleans to pray for the Society. Br. James Joseph Remich, SJ died on February 20, 2012 at the age of ninety-two and a Jesuit for fifty-two years. In his obituary it was stated: "Those who lived and worked with Brother Remich saw in him a model of faithful service and dedication to religious life."

Br. Francis J. Riedinger, SJ
1915 – 2004

Frank Riedinger was born on January 3, 1915 in a small village near Baden-Baden, Germany. Threatened by Hitler, the Riedinger family emigrated to Chicago in 1927. Because Frank was observed to be mechanically inclined, his parents enrolled him in a technical school. Radio-electronics grabbed his attention, and so he took a year-long course at the RCA Institute to obtain both the FCC Radiotelegraph and Radiotelephone commercial licenses. By 1941 Frank was employed in New Orleans.

Frank applied to be a Brother in the New Orleans Province in 1946. During his Novitiate at Grand Coteau, La, he met Fr. Frank Benedetto, SJ, who was then being assigned to Loyola University New Orleans to teach Physics. Together they discovered that Br. Frank would be an excellent fit for Loyola because of his radio-elec-

tronic skills and his machine shop experience. In 1958 he joined Tony Maurillo, the machinist of Loyola's Physics Department, where low-temperature research was getting under way. Father Frank Benedetto asked Brother Frank to learn as much as he could about cryogenics, because he wanted the lab to liquefy helium. So Frank made a tour of all the companies and universities which made liquefied helium. With a trunk load of information, Frank returned to Loyola to join with a new machinist, who together with him designed and built a helium liquefier. Their older machine, donated to the department in 1953, was itself donated to the Smithsonian Museum. Although only 16 years old, that liquefier was considered as significant in its field as the McCormack reaper and the Wright Brothers' airplane.

Frank's machine worked with such success that Loyola could supply surplus liquid helium to others. But expanding commercial production reduced the demand for liquid helium, thus the project at Loyola softened. Another Jesuit Brother, Terry Todd, SJ, learned from Frank how to manage the helium machine. Frank himself saw an advertisement for a man to repair a small island-hopping ship for the Jesuit missions in the Caroline Islands. He indeed made the ship functional for years. Later Frank volunteered to work in a Jesuit-operated warehouse in Fremont, Calif, where another Jesuit Brother had stored radio equipment for use in the Pacific missions. Frank began to repair this equipment and even to develop it for specific uses in the missions.

Frank's last months were marked by an inability to rest; a state of confusion found him trying to communicate with his care givers in German. Near Frank was Brother Terry Todd, SJ, a long-time friend, a co-worker with Frank at Loyola, and fellow missionary in the Pacific. It was fitting that Br. Francis J. Riedinger, SJ, who died returning to New Orleans after a hurricane scare, was carried off the bus in Terry's arms on September 17, 2004. Br. Francis J. Riedinger, SJ was eighty-nine years old and a Jesuit for nearly sixty years. Terry described Frank as of a gentle and kind nature; he noted Frank's quiet and extremely profitable habit of converting every scrap of leftover metal into funds for the missions.

Br. Julian Bringier Rivet, SJ
1923 – 1985

"Burt" Rivet was born in New Orleans on January 4, 1923. He was variously educated at Holy Name of Jesus, Alcee Fortier High School and St. Aloysius High School. He entered the Order at Grand Coteau, La on April 25, 1939. Burt remained there for eight years after pronouncing his vows. He was then sent to Spring Hill College in Mobile, Ala where he did the following tasks: sacristan of St. Joseph's chapel, infirmarian, refectorian, painter, worker in wood (1948-58). "Painter" should be taken as artistic painting, a warm up for his later work. He was then posted to El Paso, Texas, seven years at the new Jesuit High School and an eighth year at Sacred Heart Parish (1959-66). At the high school he served as its buyer, assistant tailor, receptionist and painter. Within a year he was made supervisor of the renovation and repair of the Jesuit residence. This man of maturity was assigned as the beadle of the brothers and scholastics at the high school. His last year in El Paso was spent at the riverside parish, Sacred Heart, from which he continued his renovation work at the high school, and served as the moderator of the art students at the Youth Center, and shepherd of the St. John Berchman's society.

He returned to Spring Hill College now as a student of art (1972), where he earned his degree, and was then posted to Jesuit College Prep in Dallas, Texas, where from 1973 until 1985, he served as a teacher of art on the faculty. These were Burt's golden years, now that he was allowed to let his talents flow freely and to engage in his unique way the students to whom he taught the zest and craft of art. A glorious twelve years it was for him, punctuated by one by-pass surgery, but felled by a second one. On July 22, 1985, Br. Julian Bringier Rivet, SJ died, sixty-two years old and forty-six years a Jesuit Brother.

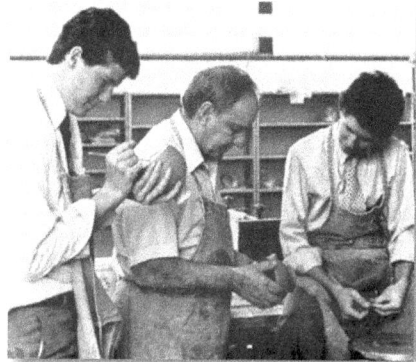

We are fortunate to have eulogies and funeral sermons about Burt, from which we excerpt these remarks. "It was quickly clear he made us all to feel, at one time or another, that we were one of the more important persons in his life." All knew him to be an iconoclast with little tolerance for airs, especially of persons in authority; he was famous for his mock fury. Even with his bluster, he was a comic figure, as when he wore a sweat shirt demanding "Support your local Brother" or "If vegetables were saints, Red Beans and Rice would be canonized." He once said, "When I first asked for special studies, I was told, 'But, Brother, you are *too young* for special studies.' Then later when I asked again, I was told, 'But, Brother, you are *too old* for special studies.' Somewhere in there I got lost."

Br. Patrick Michael Rosenblath, SJ
1928 – 1973

Patrick Michael Rosenblath was born in Mobile, Ala on August 6, 1928 of Quinlan and Mildred Rosenblath. We have no record of his education, but he entered the Society of Jesus on October 27, 1945 as a Brother novice, and took his vows on May 16, 1948. He remained at Grand Coteau, La, presumably learning his trade and craft. His first assignment was to the Jesuit House of Studies in Mobile, Ala, where for four years he was in charge of the kitchen: refectorian, supervisor of the kitchen and cook. He was sent to Jesuit High School in El Paso, Texas, now assigned as the school registrar and as moderator of the Radio and Photography Clubs. "Rosey," as his peers called him, spent one year in Shreveport, La (1967-1968), again as supervisor of the kitchen and other jobs as well. He spent just one year at Lake Dallas Retreat House in Texas as its Minister and Treasurer (1968-1969), before he returned to El Paso for three years as Minister and part of the team for CCD and CYO. Finally he took up his duties at Spring Hill College from 1972 until his death. Br. Patrick Michael Rosenblath, SJ. died in Mobile on May 19, 1973 at the age of forty-four and twenty-eight years a Jesuit Brother.

Br. Walsh Edmund Roth, SJ
1904 – 1981

Br. Edmund Roth (right)
with Br. Joseph Eaton

Walsh Edmund Roth was born in New Orleans on April 17, 1904. Edmund, as he liked to be called, attended Jesuit High School (1918-1924) and Loyola University (1925-1927). After this he became a registered pharmacist (1927-1933). Very soon after he entered the Novitiate at Grand Coteau, La on August 16, 1933 as a Brother. Much of his apostolic ministry was spent as infirmarian to various Jesuit communities. He began his infirmarian duties at Grand Coteau where he stayed from 1933 until 1937. He was moved to Jesuit High New Orleans as both infirmarian and kitchen manager (1937-1939). He was off to Spring Hill College in Mobile, Ala in the same capacity (1939-1943), after which he returned to Grand Coteau for four years (1943-1947). He moved back to Loyola University as sacristan (1947-1953). But Walsh returned to Mobile as infirmarian at the Jesuit House of Studies (1954-1956). In 1959 he traveled to the Jesuit High community in El Paso, Texas, where he remained for twenty-two years until his death in 1981.

Marty Elsner, SJ, who delivered the homily at Walsh's funeral, talked about aspects of his life that were not readily apparent. For example, Walsh used a number of sayings which tell us how he approached life. On the occasion of an auto accident he was want to say "Well, that's it. See?" This meant that he had warned us all before, but we did not listen to him. He could not eat spicy foods, but in El Paso, one could hardly avoid it. Hence, when he looked at the food, he was want to say, "What am I going to eat?"

He was an undemanding person who seemed not to ask for much nor require much. He had serious arthritis and limped as he walked, but spoke about it only when asked. The El Paso Jesuits described Walsh as a quiet and shy man who was slow to make friends. Clearly he wanted friendships, but a person approaching him had to give a bit of himself to strike up this friendship. This shy man seemed unable to invite himself to go with a group from the community; even if he wanted to go to athletic contests, for example, he needed an invitation. But invite him they did and he went with them. The conclusion of his obituary says it all: "Jesuits who lived with Walsh, especially if they took the time to create a friendship, are very happy to have been with him. He gave a consistent, loyal love, and the seeing Jesuit could notice this." On April 6, 1981, Br. Walsh Edmund Roth, SJ died at the age of seventy-six and forty-eight years as a Jesuit Brother.

Br. Joseph Holmes Smith, SJ
1908 – 1959

J. Holmes Smith was born in James, Ga on August 9, 1908. He entered the New Orleans province at Grand Coteau, La on October 14, 1926. After vows, he remained a year more at Grand Coteau, and then he spent four years at the high school in New Orleans (1930-34) seeking the best fit for his talents and the needs of the province. He was made the custodian of the clothing supplies, sacristan and receptionist. When he returned to Grand Coteau, he served as the refectorian for eight years, as

well as the brother who attended to the various needs of the college (1934-42). He went back to Jesuit High New Orleans for six years, basically continuing his previous assignments, refectorian and receptionist (1943-49). After three years back at Grand Coteau in the same jobs (1949-52), he found himself at the Jesuit House of Studies in Mobile, Ala for the rest of his life, namely, eight years, continuing the same tasks that he had done for most of his life (1953-59). He was apparently cognitively impaired, but he managed to remember the birthdays of everyone in the province. And he was a truly accomplished handball player. Br. Joseph Holmes Smith, SJ died on November 15, 1959 at the young age of fifty-one and thirty-three years as a Jesuit Brother.

Br. Hilliard F. Stiegler, SJ
1926 – 1999

Hilliard was born in New Orleans on August 4, 1926. He was educated at Holy Name grade school and St. Aloysius High School. He entered the Order as a priesthood candidate in September of 1943. After his Novitiate, he did two years of undergraduate studies, known as the Juniorate (1945-47). For some reason unknown to us, he then took his first year of regency at Jesuit High School in Tampa , Fla (1948), where he taught Latin and English. He got back on track when he went to Spring Hill College in Mobile, Ala for philosophy studies (1949-51). He had a second year of regency in Shreveport, La, where he taught English and history, as well as moderating several student activities (1952).

At this point Hilliard changed grades, from priesthood candidate to that of Brother. Back at Grand Coteau, he began his brother's work by being librarian (1953). Because he quickly displayed organizational talent, he became the buyer for the house, the czar of its kitchen, the custodian of the wine cellar and assistant treasurer (1954-58). At Spring Hill College he performed the same tasks, but when he moved across the campus to the Jesuit House of Studies, he was its buyer and refectorian (1959-65).

He returned to Grand Coteau where for ten years he served as sub-minister, treasurer, and house consultor (1965-75). He was posted to the provincial's residence with more sophisticated duties: Brother Minister and assistant treasurer for the province (1977-78). He was missioned to the community at Loyola University New Orleans as its Minister (1979-83). While at Loyola, he developed a thirst for social justice, especially in regard to the miserable black schools in the city. He focused on the rundown Fortier school, just blocks away, and recruited interested students in painting and repairing it.

During this time he took classes at Loyola's School of Business Administration and in 1980 he was awarded the MBA degree. Grand Coteau was never out of his sight, for he returned as its Brother Minister and the person in charge of the buildings (1984-92). During this time he branched out into community development at Grand Coteau. Hilliard was renowned for helping the workers at the college when their finances were tight; "generous" is the word one hears regularly. Every time there was a question of changing him, there was a long petition from the townspeople in opposition. But he did return to New Orleans. He was invited to work at the retirement community, Ignatius Residence, not because he needed assistance, but because he was offered a wonderful job. The superior at the Residence described this new job for him: (1) running all the birthday parties for the men; (2) organizing and running other seasonal social activities (Valentine's Day, Mardi Gras, the major Jesuit feasts); (3) organizing and running tours and excursions, including bringing some Jesuits to Loyola or Jesuit High School for a meal; (4) working with Music Therapy interns to come to Ignatius Residence and conduct music and singing lessons – a very popular activity with our men (remarks by Louis Poché, SJ about Hilliard Stiegler, SJ, March 9, 1993).

But Hilliard was by no means the *Magister Ludi*; he suffered all of his life with narcolepsy and depression. But once at Ignatius Residence he resumed his work of renovating schools and even becoming a special instructor in the New Orleans Parish schools (1994-99). But he began having serious heart problems, not the biblical "hard heart," but a hardening of the cardiac muscle which impeded oxygenating his blood. And in the end he was felled by primary amyloidosis. Br. Hilliard F. Stiegler, SJ died on March 3, 1999, seventy-two years old, and fifty-six years a Jesuit.

Br. Edward S. Tabit, SJ
1911 – 1962

Edward Tabit was born on January 10, 1911 in Lawrence, Kan. He entered the Order at Grand Coteau, La on December 14, 1937. After his Novitiate, he remained at Grand Coteau, serving as its kitchen czar and refectorian (1940-46). He began an eight-year stint in Miami, Fla as the sacristan of the church and moderator of the St. John Berchman's Society, namely, the altar boys. After a single year's service back at Grand Coteau, he returned to Miami in the same capacity he had served previously. He was then posted to Jesuit High School New Orleans as sacristan and custodian of the clothes closet and any maintenance needed (1952-1955). Finally he was posted to the House of Studies on the campus of Spring Hill College in Mobile, Ala, where he labored for seven more years as the receptionist, assistant refectorian and for whatever domestic tasks were required. On August 8, 1962, Br. Edward S. Tabit, SJ died, fifty-one years old and twenty-five as a Jesuit Brother.

Br. Terence Neal Todd, SJ
1940 – 20??

Terry Todd was born in New Orleans on April 16, 1940, the second of ten children. Both parents were school teachers, which may explain Terry's life-long quest for education. He attended Holy Name of Jesus elementary school (1946-53) and then Jesuit High School (1953-58). After grooming from Elmo Rogero, SJ, he entered the Order in Grand Coteau, La on Aug 14, 1958 as a scholastic novice, because, as he said, "I wanted a college education," a direction fostered by Pat Walsh, SJ, who turned Terry on to Shakespeare and poetry. By Christmas, he had discerned that his true vocation was to be a Jesuit Brother. Terry belonged to the new generation of Brothers whose motto could well have been "Be all that you can be." And so he learned on the job, first studying electricity in the

Milford Novitiate in Ohio (1961-63), then construction back at Grand Coteau (1963-65), then general maintenance at Jesuit High in El Paso, Texas (1965-66). Eventually he became the director of the Jesuit Brothers' Maintenance Corps (1969-71).

He was sent to Tampa, Fla ostensibly to be the sub-minister and do maintenance (1972-77). In his spare time he earned an associate's certificate in air conditioning from Hillsborough Community College and graduated from University of South Florida in Industrial Education in 1973. His training was climaxed by one year of college credits based on his excellent showing in a 13 hour test in Refrigeration in Princeton. Thus equipped, he went to Truk Island in the Federation of Micronesia (1977-78) to teach refrigeration, but spent four wonderful years doing maintenance at Xavier High School on Truk Island (1978-83). He returned to the states for three years, one year as Minister/Maintenance at Jesuit High New Orleans (1983-84) and two years in the Physics Department Laboratory at Loyola University (1984-86). The university newspaper published an article about Terry, confirming the fact that he was a man of remarkable insight.

> " This is a Collins helium cryostat," explained Br. Terry Todd, SJ, speaking with a half-drawn grin in slow but precise syllables that dropped heavily to the concrete floor. The cryostat, an apparatus which helps convert helium from gas to liquid, has a niche in what Todd describes as his domain – the winding machine shop and physics laboratory in Monroe Hall. The burly brother works primarily in cryogenics, a branch of the physical sciences which deals with the production of very low temperatures. Todd said that the liquid helium he manufactures is used for experiments in the Loyola science community. Specifically, physics professors David Keiffer and Creston King are employing it in a joint project with Alabama Cryogenic Engineering to design a space refrigerator for NASA. … Todd considers his work to be a dynamic learning process. He has done everything from simple electric wiring to rebuilding whole cars from baskets of parts. Cryogenics, undertaken in August of 1983, is only his most recent foray into the technical world, and he is still a new comer at it. Last month the cryostat machine broke down, and Todd had to repair it. Never having attempted such a task, he had only the directions and diagrams of manuals to guide him. He succeeded and professors King and Keiffer threw him a champagne party in celebration. "Fixing the cryostat was a major achievement for me … I find my new work very exciting." (from the October 25, 1985 edition of the *Loyola Maroon*).

Terry returned to Micronesia and remained there for seventeen years (1986-2003). First he was posted to the Pohnpei Agricultural and Trade School on the island, where he ruled and guided as Asst. Director, Plant Manager, Coordinator of the Jesuits' Assoc. Program. In an interview, Terry commented on his desire to learn everything: "I like to think of myself as a type of renaissance man. I'm not just interested in refrigeration. Brother Anthony Coco taught me a lot about mechanics … I understand a lot about a lot of different types of machines, but I still think if I would not have gone to the islands, my skills would be a lot more specialized. I would not have had the opportunity to learn so many different aspect of mechanics."

Like the absent father in *The Glass Menagerie*, Terry was in love with "long distances," places far away. He offered himself for the missions, both Sri Lanka and Africa, but settled comfortably to the Caroline Islands for many years. Terry is notorious for long bike rides and an assault on the Appalachian Trail. To finish this, Terry and his mother eventually took a 2,500 mile trip.

At his departure from the islands, Terry was feted and lauded at the graduation of the Jesuit High School there. Besides the usual testimonials, he was said to have a "third eye," that is, a forward vision to imagine things ahead. Terry returned to the Province in 2003 for a sabbatical. For the next ten years he dwelt at Ignatius Residence in New Orleans and at Loyola University. He became the minister of Ignatius Residence, as well as a physics lab technician at the University across the river. Ignatius Residence was most fortunate to have Terry there because he put fizz in their drinks, took some of them to Perdido Villa for fun and games, and generally brought his largeness to the community. In short, he was the Terry we all knew and admired. He was known to quote Shakespeare and poetry *en pointe* at meals and in conversation; he prided himself on his foresight to take lots of books with him to Micronesia, all of which he ultimately read.

We report this incident because so many of Terry's virtues are on display here. The Ignatius Residence community in New Orleans fled Hurricane Ivan in 2004 and camped at Our Lady of the Oaks in Grand Coteau, La until it was time to go home. On the return trip, Br. Frank Riedinger, SJ apparently died on the bus. And when the bus arrived, it was Terry who entered and carried Frank's corpse out and laid it reverently inside the compound. They had been lifelong friends and corresponded frequently.

When Ignatius Residence moved to Grand Coteau to become the St. Alphonsus Pavilion, he remained in New Orleans as caretaker of the property, and eventually moved to Jesuit High New Orleans to join the Maintenance Department. In his own words, he stated that Luke 9:62 has been very influential in his lifetime: "'No man putting his hand to the plow and looking back is fit for the kingdom of God.' This may not be good advice for everyone, but it has been a substantial help to me along the way." A Brother with a "third eye."

Br. Oscar Patrick Usina, SJ
1923 – 1981

Oscar Patrick Usina was born in St. Augustine, Fla on May 14, 1923. Pat received all of his education in St. Augustine, first at the Cathedral Parochial School (1928-36) and at St. Joseph Academy high school (1936-40). On August 14, 1941 "Pat," never "Oscar,"entered the Society of Jesus at the Novitiate in Grand Coteau, La. He entered as a candidate for priesthood, and so certain studies were job-specific: two years of Juniorate (1943-45), three years at Spring Hill College in Mobile, Ala studying philosophy, during which Pat earned a B.S. degree in physics (1947). Regency followed with one year at Spring Hill and one year at Jesuit High in Dallas, Texas. During this time he discerned that Jesuit priesthood was not his vocation, but being a Jesuit definitely was. Hence Pat transferred to the grade of temporal coadjutor and officially became a Brother on August 18, 1950.

He went to work immediately in the treasurer's office at Grand Coteau (1950-54). He joined the Provincial's staff at Jesuit High New Orleans as assistant treasurer (1954-57). And from there he went to Xavier Hall Retreat House in Pass Christian, Miss, for two years as its bookkeeper. He spent one year at Grand Coteau before he settled down in 1960 for twenty-one years at Jesuit College Prep in Dallas as its treasurer. Along the way he picked up a nickname, "Louch," the meaning of which seems to have died with him.

Pat Usina was one of those people who seem easily accessible. He received a lot of teasing, but this meant to him that his community noticed him. We will never know how his lisp affected his life, but he was fearless in trying to communicate. He was genuinely good to be with; he made friends, even Jesuits, easily. His change of grades from priest candidate to Brother seemed to be an obvious and wise decision. As bookkeeper and as a province financial examiner, he was superb, even to the point of telling the Provincial on one occasion that "they say they have xxx dollars, but I can't find it." As his health began to fail, he was assigned to the province infirmary in New Orleans. On August 10, 1981 Br. Oscar Patrick Usina, SJ died, at the age of fifty-eight and forty years a Jesuit Brother.

Front Row: Brs. Elliott, Roth, Cabral, Gavan, Tabit
Back Row: Brs. Stiegler, Riedinger, Hinze, Smith, Usina, Lee Phillips, Nowak, Mock, Fr. Bob Nilon
circa 1957

Patient Trust

Trust in the slow work of God.
We are quite naturally impatient
  in everything to reach the end
  without delay.
We should like to skip
  all intermediate stages.
We are impatient of being
  on the way to something,
  unknown, something new.
Yet it is the law that all progress
  is made by passing through
  some stages of instability.
And so I think it is with you,
  your ideas mature gradually
   – let them grow,
   – let them shape themselves,
    without undue haste.
Do not try to force them,
 as though you could be today what time
 (that is to say, grace and circumstances
 acting on your own good will)
 will make of you tomorrow.
Only God could say what this new spirit
  gradually forming within you will be.
Give Our Lord the benefit of believing
  That his hand is leading you,
And accept the anxiety of feeling yourself
  In suspense and incomplete

— Pierre Teilhard de Chardin, SJ.

Art by Brother Burt Rivet, SJ

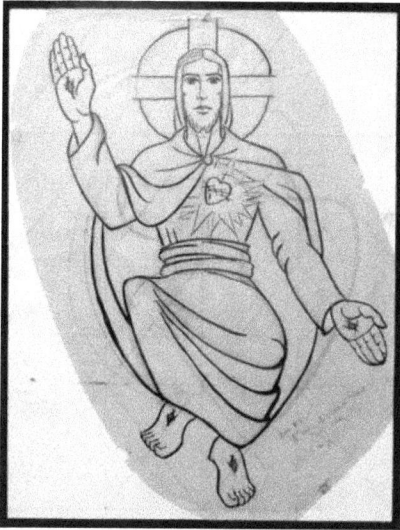

Sketch for Sacred Heart
Pencil on Paper

Sacred Heart
Wrought Iron

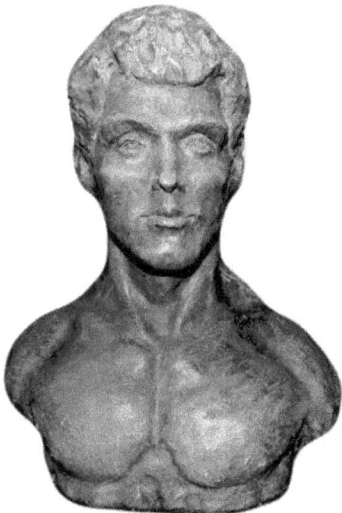

Bust of an Athlete
Ceramic

Madonna and Child
Bronze

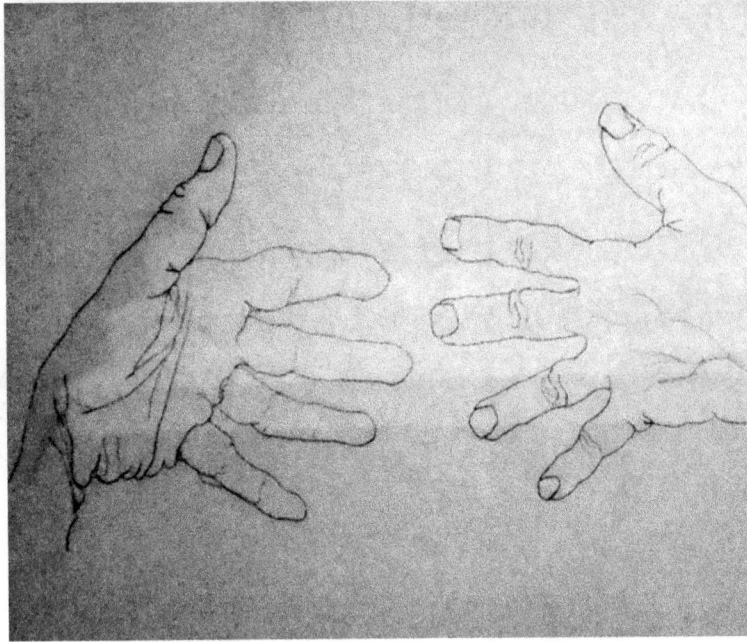

Hands Study
Pencil on paper

Figure Study
Oil pastel and wash

Wine Bottles
Acrylic on Canvus

Nuns
Pencil and Charcoal

Our Lady of Guadalupe
Oil

Art by Brother Gebhard Fröhlich, SJ

Icon of the Christ
Tempera & gold leaf on wood

St. Catherine of Siena
Acrylic

St. Clare of Assisi
Acrylic

St. Francis of Assisi
Acrylic

Br. Gebhard Fröhlich, SJ

St. Alphonsus Rodriguez, SJ
Oil on canvus

Circa 1955   1st row: Brs. Maitland, Phillips, Federovich, Rosenblath, Elliot
2nd row: Brs. S. Schott, Bryan, Usina, Nowak, Lonergan, Lapeyre, Collison
3rd row: Brs. Cunningham, Gavan, Roth, Rivet, Henderson, Burges
4th row: Brs. ??, Barry, Arrizabalaga, Cody, Riedinger, ??, Donellan
5th row: Br. Hinze, Fr. Larion Elliot, Br. Stiegler, Fr. Fuss, Br. Smith, Fr. Burleigh, ??

Brs. Arrizabalaga, Barry, Blank, Booth, Bray, Burges, Coco, Cody, Collison, Cunningham, DeLaHoussaye,
Doherty, Donellan, Eckler, Federovich, Ferlita, Gelpi, Gravois, Hinze, Landry, Lapeyre, Lavergne, Lonergan,
Maitland, Martin, Mock, Moore, Ory, Remich, Riedinger, Rivet, Rosenblath, Stiegler, Timmerman, Usina, *et alii*
Circa 1962

Seated & kneeling: Brs. Blank, Concha, Remich, Todd, Phillips, Eckler, Elliot, Barry, Stiegler, Landry, Ardoin, Dardis, Ory, Salcido, Federovich, Coco, DeLaHoussaye, Blouin

Standing: Brs. Maitland, Korte, Booth, Glancy, Bray, Hinze, Gravois, Lonergan, Ferlita, Timmerman, Gussio, Duco, Usina, S. Schott, Gelpi, Burges, Donellan, Fr. Robert Nilon, Brs. Arrizabalaga, Conner, Riedinger, Doherty, Burleigh, Cunningham

October, 1964

120

Kneeling: Brs. Remich, DeLaHoussaye, Riedinger, ??, Ory, Lapeyre, Gavan, Cabral, Stiegler,
Martin, Booth, Cody, Standish, Roth, Fr. Tonnar, Br. Dardis

Standing: Brs. Maitland, Timmerman, Collison, Doherty, Gravois, Usina, Waltz, Hinze, Gussio,
Landry, Mock, Lonergan, Eckler, Nowak, Donellan, ??, S. Schott, Bryan, Coco, Buckman, Rivet

Circa 1966

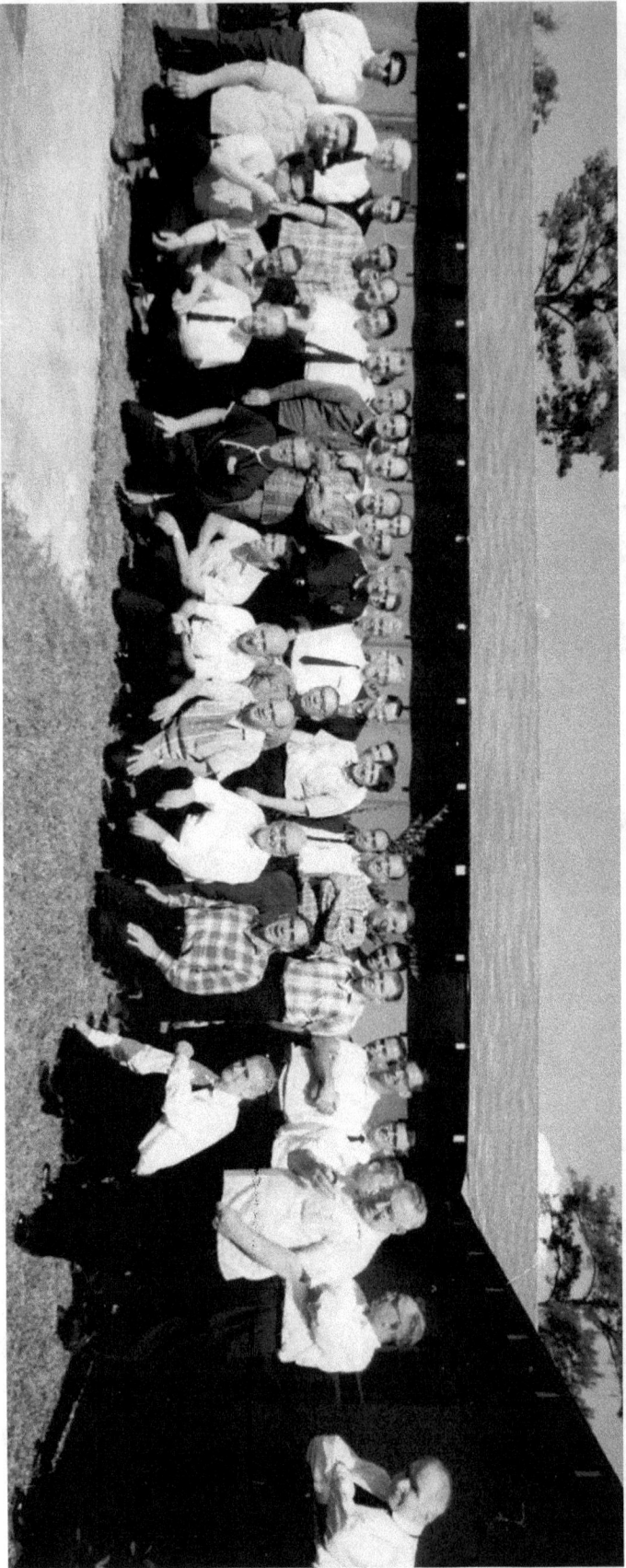

Kneeling: Brs. Lonergan, ??, Landry, Gavan, ??, ??, Remich, Nowak, Elliot, Hinze, Barry, Bryan
Standing: Brs. Concha, Collison, Gelpi, Ardoin, Moore, Rivet, Maitland, Cody, ??, Glancy, Booth,??, Stiegler,
??, Doherty, Mock, Fr. Keller, ??, ??, Usina, ??, Lapeyre, Fr. Koch, Gravois, Greer, Coco, Blank,
S. Schott, Ferlita, Dardis, Fr. Wiltz, ??, Walz, Duco, Cunningham, Fr. Edwards, Bray
Circa 1970

122

1st Row: Brs. Murphy, Hinze, Fr. Buddendorff, Booth, Stiegler, Lonergan, Nowak, Fr. Rodriguez, Lapeyre, Feltes, Fr. Fabacher, Fr. Hypolite
2nd Row: Brs. Puza, Todd, Blank, Donellan, Moore, Riedinger, Barry, Gussio, Scherman, Mr. Gallagher, Fr. Doyle, Eckler, Fröhlich, Fr. Alchediak
3rd Row: Fr. Wiltz, Brs. Ferlita, Gossett, Martin, Lundin, Dardis, ??, Doherty, Ory, Landry, Elliot, Cabral, Remich, Fr. Postell, Fr. Keller

Circa 1984

Seated: Brs. Donellan, Murphy, Barry
Standing: Moore, Scherman, Stiegler, Lonergan
Circa 1984

Seated: Brs. Hinze, Feltes, Nowak
Standing: Lapeyre, Booth
Circa 1984

Seated: Brs. Dardis, Huck, Puza, Eckler, Coco
Standing: Ferlita, Fröhlich, Lundin, Todd, Martin, Blank
Feast of St. Alphonsus Rodriguez, October 2012

Briefest of Bibliographies

Biever, Albert Hubert, SJ
   The Jesuits in New Orleans and the Mississippi Valley. 1924.

Burrus, Ernest J., SJ
   "Jesuits Came Late, but Built Up El Paso for 100 Years," *Southern Jesuit,* v. 1. Dec. 1981, Catholic Archives of Texas, Austin TX.

Clancy, Thomas Henley, SJ
   "The Ante-Bellum Jesuits of the New Orleans Province," *Louisiana History* v. 25. 1993, pp. 327-433.
   "Jesuits in the South: The Last 150 years," *The Southern Jesuit, v.* 2. 1982, pp. 9-30.
   Our Friends, 1st edition: 1978; 2nd edition: 1989; 3rd edition: 1999.

Delanglez, Jean, SJ
   The Jesuits in Lower Louisiana. New Orleans: Loyola University Press, 1935.

Dunne, Peter Masten, SJ
   Pioneer Jesuits in Northern Mexico. Los Angeles: UC Press, 1944.

Kenny, Michael, SJ
   Jesuits in Our Southland 1566-1946. Origin and Growth of New Orleans Province. Kenny Papers, Loyola University New Orleans, 1946.

O'Neill, Charles E., SJ
   Diccionario histórico de la Compania de Jesús. 4 volumns, Rome: Institute of History of the Society of Jesus, 2001.

Owens, Sister Lilliana, SL
   Carlos M. Pinto, SJ. El Paso: Revista Catolica Press, 1951.

Ryan, Stephen P., SJ
   Jesuits, The Handbook of Texas Online. Texas State History Association, June 15, 2010.

Stansell, Harold L. SJ
   Regis: on the Crest of the West. Denver: Regis Educational Corporation, 2003.

Woodstock Letters

Young, Janine
   "Jesuits Have Long History in El Paso's Catholic Community." *The Times,* 03/25/2013.

Only in God

Only in God will my soul be at rest
From Him comes my hope, my salvation.
God alone is my rock of safety,
My strength, my Glory, my God.

Trust in God at all times, O people,
And pour out your hearts.
God Himself is a refuge for us
And a stronghold for our fears.

Many times have I heard God tell
Of His long lasting love.
You, Yourself, Lord reward all who labor
For love of Your Name.

- John Foley, SJ

INDEX

ISBN   13:978-0692620281

www.ingramcontent.com/pod-product-compliance
Lightning Source LLC
Chambersburg PA
CBHW081011040426
42443CB00016B/3484